Copyright © 2023 by Trient Press

All rights reserved. No part of this publication may be reproduced, distributed, or transmitted in any form or by any means, including photocopying, recording, or other electronic or mechanical methods, without the prior written permission of the publisher, except in the case of brief quotations embodied in critical reviews and certain other noncommercial uses permitted by copyright law. For permission requests, write to the publisher, addressed "Attention: Permissions Coordinator," at the address below.

Criminal copyright infringement, including infringement without monetary gain, is investigated by the FBI and is punishable by up to five years in federal prison and a fine of $250,000.

Except for the original story material written by the author, all songs, song titles, and lyrics mentioned in the novel Echoes of Eternity: Exploring Ancient Babylon's Rituals are the exclusive property of the respective artists, songwriters, and copyright holder.

Trient Press
3375 S Rainbow Blvd
#81710, SMB 13135
Las Vegas, NV 89180

Ordering Information:
Quantity sales. Special discounts are available on quantity purchases by corporations, associations, and others. For details, contact the publisher at the address above.
Orders by U.S. trade bookstores and wholesalers. Please contact Trient Press: Tel: (775) 996-3844; or visit www.trientpress.com.

Printed in the United States of America

Publisher's Cataloging-in-Publication data
Ruscsak, M.L.
A title of a book : Echoes of Eternity: Exploring Ancient Babylon's Rituals
ISBN

Hard Cover	979-8-88990-118-1
Paper Back	979-8-88990-119-8
Ebook	979-8-88990-120-4

Chapter 1 Rituals

Chapter 2 Incantations

Chapter 3 Spells

Chapter 4 Unveiling the Shadows

Exploring Ancient Babylon's Rituals

Welcome to "Echoes of Eternity: Exploring Ancient Babylon's Rituals, Incantations, Spells, and Unveiling the Shadows." Within the pages of this comprehensive guide, we embark on a captivating journey through the mystical tapestry of ancient Babylonian practices, unearthing the rituals, incantations, and spells that shaped their vibrant and enigmatic civilization.

Chapter 1 initiates our exploration into the world of rituals. Discover the sacred ceremonies and symbolic acts that formed the foundation of Babylonian spiritual life. From elaborate temple rites to personal rituals, we delve into the significance of these practices and the role they played in connecting with the divine.

In Chapter 2, we turn our attention to the power of incantations. Explore the mystical art of spoken words and the incantations that carried the hopes, fears, and desires of the Babylonians. Learn how these carefully crafted utterances were believed to channel supernatural forces and bring about change in the physical and spiritual realms.

Chapter 3 takes us deeper into the realm of spells. Unlock the secrets of ancient Babylonian spellcraft, as we unravel the enchantments and invocations that were utilized for various purposes. Unleash the potential of these ancient formulas and uncover the hidden wisdom they hold.

Finally, in Chapter 4, we delve into the shadows, unveiling the darker aspects of Babylonian spirituality. Here, we explore the forbidden arts, the boundaries crossed, and the inherent risks associated with practices such as soul manipulation, blood magic, and forbidden rituals. Delve into the depths of ancient Babylon's dark magic and witness the delicate balance between power and consequence.

Throughout our journey, we draw upon the expertise of renowned scholars and delve into ancient texts to provide you with a comprehensive understanding of these esoteric practices. We encourage you to approach this study with reverence, respect, and a commitment to ethical exploration.

"Echoes of Eternity: Exploring Ancient Babylon's Rituals, Incantations, Spells, and Unveiling the Shadows" invites you to peer into the rich tapestry of Babylonian mysticism. As we uncover their ancient wisdom, we embrace the echoes of a civilization that once flourished and left an indelible mark on the annals of human history.

Let us embark on this profound journey together, as we step back in time and unlock the secrets of ancient Babylon's rituals, incantations, spells, and the enigmatic shadows that lie beneath.

Exploring Ancient Babylon's Rituals

Chapter 1

Rituals:

Exploring Ancient Babylon's Rituals

The Purification of the Sacred Temple

In the ancient realm of Babylon, the Purification of the Sacred Temple was a revered ritual, undertaken with great reverence and meticulous attention to detail. It was a solemn ceremony that aimed to cleanse the temple's sacred space and restore its harmonious connection to the divine forces.

As the dawn light broke upon the sacred city of Babylon, its inhabitants prepared for the sacred rite known as the Purification of the Sacred Temple. The High Priest, adorned in flowing ceremonial robes embellished with intricate symbols, led a procession of temple priests and priestesses through the bustling streets. The air was thick with anticipation and reverence, for this was a momentous occasion, a chance to renew the bond between mortals and the gods.

Upon reaching the towering gates of the temple, they were swung open, revealing the magnificent courtyard within. The courtyard, adorned with vibrant flowers and ornate statues, basked in the gentle glow of the morning sun. A hushed silence fell upon the gathered crowd as they awaited the commencement of the sacred ritual.

The High Priest ascended the marble steps that led to the temple's entrance, each footfall resonating with purpose. At the threshold, he raised his hands high, invoking the blessings of the divine pantheon. With a voice that resonated like thunder, he recited ancient invocations, calling upon the gods to grant their presence and blessing.

As the sacred words echoed through the temple, a procession of acolytes brought forth vases filled with pure water drawn from the sacred springs. Each vessel was delicately decorated with intricate carvings depicting the deities. With utmost care, the High Priest dipped a ceremonial brush into the water, symbolizing the sacred cleansing to come.

The High Priest, accompanied by his attendants, proceeded to move through the temple's hallowed halls, meticulously anointing the statues and altars, the sacred relics and symbols of power, with the consecrated water. He chanted ancient incantations, invoking the ancient spirits of purity and sanctity to cleanse and restore the temple's divine connection.

The consecrated water, a symbol of divine purification, was gently sprinkled upon the temple's floors, washing away any lingering impurities and negativities that may have accumulated. As the droplets of water landed upon the ground, they shimmered like liquid sunlight, carrying the essence of divine blessings.

The purification ritual continued for hours, with every nook and corner of the temple receiving the sanctifying touch of the High Priest's brush and the cleansing cascade of the sacred water. Each action was imbued with intention and devotion, aimed at revitalizing the spiritual essence that permeated the sacred space.

As the final anointing was completed, the High Priest stood before the congregation, his voice rising in a powerful crescendo. He thanked the gods for their presence, acknowledging their benevolence and wisdom. He beseeched them to grant their continued favor upon the temple and its devotees, ensuring prosperity, protection, and enlightenment.

With the ritual drawing to a close, the High Priest raised his arms high, signaling the conclusion of the sacred ceremony. The gathered worshippers erupted into a chorus of praises and hymns, their voices intertwining with the swirling incense and the fading echoes of the High Priest's words.

From that moment forward, the temple stood as a bastion of divine purity, ready to welcome worshippers seeking solace, guidance, and communion with the gods. The Purification of the Sacred Temple had not only cleansed the physical space but had also rekindled the celestial connection, a bond woven through the fabric of time, uniting the earthly and the divine in sacred harmony.

If this was performed today:

If the Purification of the Sacred Temple were to be performed today, it would require careful preparation and adherence to the essence and symbolism of the ancient Babylonian ritual. While the original words and specific practices may be lost to time, the following is a suggested adaptation that captures the spirit of the ancient rite:

Preparation:

Choose a date and time for the purification ritual, preferably during a significant celestial event or an auspicious period.
Gather the temple priests and priestesses who will participate in the ritual.
Select ceremonial garments and adornments that reflect the sacredness of the occasion.

Sanctifying the Temple Grounds:

Cleanse the temple grounds by sweeping away physical debris and purifying the area with sacred herbs or incense.
Prepare an altar at the heart of the temple, adorned with symbolic representations of the gods and sacred artifacts.
Arrange ritual tools, such as a ceremonial brush, vases for water, and any additional items specific to your tradition.

Invoking the Divine Presence:

Begin the ritual at dawn or a designated time, aligning with the sacred energy of the new day.
The High Priest, dressed in ceremonial robes, leads a procession of temple priests and priestesses through the temple grounds, carrying lit candles or lamps to symbolize the divine light.

Opening the Temple Gates:

As the procession reaches the temple gates, they are ceremonially opened to symbolize the welcoming of the gods and the connection between the mortal and divine realms.

Invocations and Prayers:

The High Priest stands before the temple entrance and raises their hands high, invoking the blessings and presence of the gods.
Recite ancient invocations, prayers, or hymns that honor the deities and express gratitude for their benevolence and wisdom.

Anointing with Purified Water:

A procession of temple acolytes brings vases filled with pure water, drawn from sacred springs or consecrated sources.
The High Priest dips a ceremonial brush into the water, symbolizing the sacred cleansing to come.

Ritual Cleansing of the Temple:

The High Priest, accompanied by their attendants, moves through the hallowed halls and chambers of the temple.
Meticulously anoint statues, altars, sacred relics, symbols of power, and every corner of the temple with the consecrated water.

Chant ancient incantations or prayers, invoking the spirits of purity and sanctity to cleanse and restore the temple's divine connection.

Purification of the Temple Floors:

The consecrated water, symbolizing divine purification, is gently sprinkled upon the temple floors.
This act washes away any lingering impurities and negativities that may have accumulated, purifying the sacred space.

Closing the Ritual:

The High Priest stands before the gathered congregation, expressing gratitude to the gods for their presence and blessings.
Pray for the gods' continued favor upon the temple and its devotees, seeking prosperity, protection, and enlightenment.

Conclusion:

The High Priest raises their arms high, signaling the conclusion of the sacred ceremony.
The gathered worshippers erupt into a chorus of praises and hymns, their voices intertwining with the fading echoes of the High Priest's words.
Post-Ritual:

The temple remains sanctified and ready to welcome worshippers seeking solace, guidance, and communion with the gods.
Maintain the sacredness of the temple by periodically performing smaller purification rituals or maintenance tasks as needed.

The Summoning of the Celestial Guardians

In the ancient realm of Babylon, the Summoning of the Celestial Guardians was a solemn and awe-inspiring ritual, conducted to invoke the celestial forces and seek their protection and guidance. Enshrouded in mystic incantations and surrounded by the ethereal glow of starlight, this sacred rite connected mortals to the celestial realm. Here is a description of this ritual, immersed in the tone of ancient Babylon:

As twilight settled over the celestial canopy, the city of Babylon grew still, preparing for the sacred rite known as the Summoning of the Celestial Guardians. The High Astrologer, adorned in flowing robes adorned with intricate constellations, stood atop the grand ziggurat, its peak reaching towards the heavens. Around him, a circle of disciples and initiates formed, their eyes alight with anticipation.

Above, the velvety tapestry of the night sky unfurled, adorned with shimmering stars that seemed to dance in celestial unison. The High Astrologer raised his arms, his voice carrying across the hushed gathering, calling upon the celestial forces with ancient invocations, words that bridged the realms of mortals and gods.

With each incantation, the air grew charged with mystical energy. The disciples, their hearts pounding, joined the High Astrologer, their voices blending into a resonant chant that reverberated through the darkness. The celestial language of the gods echoed through the night, a symphony of power and reverence.

As the chant reached its crescendo, the High Astrologer extended a hand towards the heavens, fingers outstretched in supplication. And in response, the twinkling stars seemed to shift and gather, aligning in constellations that mirrored the ancient symbols etched upon the temple walls.

From the celestial realms, luminous beings descended, their radiant forms aglow with otherworldly energy. These were the Celestial Guardians, entrusted with the task of safeguarding the mortal realm from malevolent forces and bestowing their divine wisdom upon those deemed worthy. Each guardian bore a unique presence, embodying the essence of a specific celestial body.

The High Astrologer, his voice a whisper, spoke words of gratitude and reverence to the celestial visitors. He acknowledged their might and wisdom, acknowledging their eternal watch over the city of Babylon. In turn, the Celestial Guardians extended their ethereal hands, bestowing blessings upon the gathering below.

In a profound moment of communion, disciples and initiates stood in the presence of these divine beings, basking in their celestial radiance. The High Astrologer beseeched the guardians to lend their celestial influence, offering guidance and protection to the people of Babylon, guiding them through both prosperous times and trials.

As the final words of invocation hung in the air, the Celestial Guardians gradually ascended, their radiant forms blending seamlessly with the celestial tapestry above. The disciples and initiates stood in awe, their spirits uplifted and hearts filled with celestial blessings.

From that moment forward, the people of Babylon knew that the Celestial Guardians watched over them, their celestial presence a constant reminder of the harmonious connection between mortals and the celestial realms. The Summoning of the Celestial Guardians had forged an everlasting bond, uniting the city with the cosmic forces that governed the universe.

If this was performed today:

If the Summoning of the Celestial Guardians were to be performed today, it would require a deep reverence for the celestial realm and a connection to the mystical energy that permeates the universe. While the original words and specific practices may be lost to time, the following is a suggested adaptation that captures the essence and tone of the ancient Babylonian ritual:

Preparation:

Choose a date and time for the ritual, preferably during a celestial event such as a planetary alignment or a significant phase of the moon.
Gather a group of participants who will partake in the summoning ritual.
Select ceremonial attire or garments that evoke a sense of connection with the celestial realms.

Creating a Sacred Space:

Find or designate a suitable outdoor location where the ritual will take place, such as a clearing or a sacred grove.
Cleanse the area by removing physical debris and energetically purify it with sacred smoke or incense.

Setting up the Altar:

Arrange a central altar adorned with celestial symbols, such as representations of the planets, stars, and other celestial bodies.
Place candles or lamps around the altar to symbolize the guiding light of the celestial guardians.
Include additional tools and items specific to your tradition, such as crystals, herbs, or ritual objects associated with the celestial realms.

Invocation and Chant:

Begin the ritual at dusk or a designated time when the celestial energies are believed to be heightened.
Gather in a circle around the altar, with the High Astrologer or designated leader at the center.
Begin the summoning by leading a chant or prayer that calls upon the celestial forces and invokes the presence of the celestial guardians.
Craft a chant or prayer that resonates with your intention, expressing reverence, gratitude, and a sincere invitation to the celestial beings.

Alignment with the Celestial Energies:

The participants join in the chant or prayer, raising their voices in unison, creating a harmonic vibration that resonates with the celestial realms.
Focus on attuning your energies with the cosmic forces and opening yourselves to receive the wisdom and guidance of the celestial guardians.

Symbolic Gestures:

As the chant continues, participants may raise their arms towards the sky, symbolically reaching out to the celestial realms.
Some may choose to incorporate sacred movements, such as gentle swaying or circular motions, to further align their energies with the celestial currents.
Celestial Convergence:

As the chant reaches its climax, participants visualize the celestial energies converging and gathering above the ritual space.
Imagine the stars and planets aligning, creating a celestial bridge between the mortal realm and the realms of the guardians.

Manifestation of the Celestial Guardians:

With focused intention, envision the celestial guardians descending from the realms above, their radiant forms becoming visible to the participants.
Each guardian represents a specific celestial body, embodying its unique energy and wisdom.

Communion and Invocation of Blessings:

The High Astrologer or designated leader addresses the celestial guardians, expressing gratitude for their presence and acknowledging their divine influence.
Participants may take turns speaking words of reverence, asking for guidance, protection, and blessings from the celestial guardians.
Offerings such as incense, flowers, or symbolic items representing the celestial bodies can be presented on the altar as acts of devotion and gratitude.

Conclusion and Farewell:

Express gratitude to the celestial guardians for their presence and wisdom.
Conclude the ritual by collectively offering a final prayer or chant that acknowledges the completion of the summoning and the closing of the celestial gateway.
Slowly disperse the energy, gradually grounding yourselves by visualizing the energy flowing back into the earth.

Remember to adapt these steps and elements to align with your specific beliefs, traditions, and resources. The intention, focus, and reverence with which the ritual is performed are vital in invoking the presence of the Celestial Guardians.

The Divination of the Sacred River

As the golden rays of the Babylonian sun bathed the sacred city, the people gathered along the banks of the Euphrates River, preparing for the ancient rite known as the Divination of the Sacred River. The High Diviner, draped in garments adorned with mystical symbols, stood upon a stone platform overlooking the shimmering waters. Around him, a hushed crowd of eager onlookers awaited the revelation of destiny.

The air was thick with anticipation, for the Euphrates River was believed to hold the secrets of the gods, carrying the messages of the celestial realms to the mortal realm below. The High Diviner raised his arms, calling upon the ancient forces that governed the cosmos. His voice, like a gentle breeze, resonated with power and reverence as he chanted sacred invocations that bridged the realms of mortals and deities.

As the chants echoed through the valley, the High Diviner extended his hands toward the flowing river, beseeching the spirits of the water to reveal their hidden knowledge. The crowd watched with bated breath as the currents responded, swirling and undulating in mysterious patterns. It was as if the river itself listened and prepared to communicate the divine messages.

With each passing moment, the movements of the river grew more pronounced, taking on shapes and symbols that spoke of the future and the fates of those gathered. The High Diviner, his eyes filled with ancient wisdom, deciphered the enigmatic language of the water, interpreting the signs and symbols presented before him.

The onlookers, eager to glimpse their destinies, held their breath as the High Diviner shared his divinations. With each revelation, he spoke of fortunes and challenges, victories and trials, guiding the people along their paths and offering insights into their individual journeys.

The Divination of the Sacred River was not only a means to glimpse the future but also a moment of reflection and introspection. It was a reminder of the interconnectedness of humanity and the cosmos, as the river's movements mirrored the ebb and flow of life itself.

As the last symbol faded from the river's surface, the High Diviner lowered his arms, concluding the divination. The crowd erupted in whispers and murmurs, their hearts and minds filled with the wisdom imparted. They carried the messages of the river within their souls, ready to navigate the challenges and embrace the blessings that lay ahead.

From that moment forward, the people of Babylon walked with a heightened sense of purpose and awareness, guided by the wisdom bestowed upon them through the Divination of the Sacred River. The flowing waters had revealed glimpses of the future, reminding all that they were part of a grand tapestry woven by the gods themselves.

If this was performed today:

Preparation:

Choose a location along the banks of a sacred river, preferably during a time when the sun's rays illuminate the water, enhancing its mystical qualities.
Gather a group of participants who will take part in the divination ritual.
Select clothing or adornments that reflect reverence for the river and the divine forces it represents.

Creating a Sacred Space:

Cleanse the area near the river by removing physical debris and energetically purify it with sacred smoke or incense.
Place sacred stones or objects at the water's edge to mark the sacred space.

Invocation and Connection:

Stand or sit in a circle near the river, with the High Diviner or designated leader at the center.
Begin the ritual by leading a chant or prayer that invokes the presence and blessings of the river spirits and water deities.
Craft a chant or prayer that expresses respect, gratitude, and a sincere desire to receive guidance and wisdom from the sacred river.

Offerings and Sacred Objects:

Prepare offerings such as flowers, herbs, or small tokens that symbolize intentions or questions you wish to divine.
Each participant may hold their offering and silently infuse it with their intentions, connecting their energy with the flow of the river.

Scrying or Observation:

Encourage participants to find a comfortable spot near the riverbank and focus their gaze on the water's surface.
As the river flows, pay attention to any patterns, movements, or symbols that emerge, interpreting them as messages from the river spirits.

Questions and Intentions:

Encourage participants to silently formulate questions or intentions that they seek guidance on.
Each person takes turns approaching the water's edge, offering their question or intention to the river, and gently releasing their offering into the water.

Silence and Reflection:

After each offering, participants enter a period of silence to allow the river spirits to communicate and reveal insights.
Encourage them to quiet their minds, open their hearts, and attune to the subtle messages that may arise.

Shared Interpretation and Insights:

As the divination session concludes, gather as a group and share any visions, symbols, or impressions that were received from the river.
Engage in a collective discussion to interpret the messages and insights, offering support and guidance to one another.

Expressing Gratitude and Closing:

Offer thanks to the river spirits, water deities, and the sacred river itself for their presence and wisdom.
Conclude the ritual with a closing prayer or chant that acknowledges the completion of the divination and expresses gratitude for the guidance received.
Remember to adapt these steps and elements to align with your specific beliefs, traditions, and resources. The divination process relies on intuition, receptivity, and attunement to the river's energy and the messages it conveys.

The Festival of the New Moon

Exploring Ancient Babylon's Rituals

As the last rays of the setting sun cast a warm glow over the ancient city of Babylon, the inhabitants eagerly prepared for the grand celebration known as the Festival of the New Moon. It was a time of renewal, when the waxing crescent moon marked the beginning of a new lunar cycle and signaled the promise of abundance and prosperity.

The city streets buzzed with anticipation as merchants adorned their stalls with vibrant tapestries, exotic spices, and shimmering jewels. The air was alive with the melodies of musicians, the rhythmic beats of drums, and the laughter of children. Babylonians from all walks of life gathered in the central square, their hearts filled with hope and excitement.

The High Priestess, draped in flowing garments of celestial blue, stood at the forefront of the festivities. Her presence commanded respect and awe, for she was believed to possess a direct connection to the moon goddess, Ishtar. With a voice that carried like a gentle breeze, she led the ceremonial procession towards the sacred temple.

The procession wound its way through the city, accompanied by dancers twirling in colorful costumes and acrobats performing gravity-defying feats. The sound of tambourines and flutes filled the air, merging with the jubilant cheers of the crowd. The people waved garlands of flowers and lit fragrant incense, their offerings to the moon goddess.

Upon reaching the temple, the High Priestess ascended the grand staircase, her every movement exuding grace and reverence. At the entrance, she raised her arms to the sky, invoking the blessings of Ishtar and the celestial forces. Her voice resonated with devotion as she recited ancient prayers, beseeching the moon goddess to shower her blessings upon the city and its inhabitants.

Inside the temple, the sacred fires burned bright, illuminating the altar adorned with offerings of ripe fruits, golden wheat, and sweet honey. The air was filled with the fragrance of burning herbs and the soft glow of candlelight. The High Priestess, surrounded by temple priestesses, performed sacred rituals to honor the lunar energy and invoke its powers of fertility, growth, and harmony.

As the moon began to emerge in the night sky, its crescent silhouette casting a gentle glow, the High Priestess led the assembled crowd in chants and hymns. The rhythmic chorus reverberated through the temple, resonating with the vibrancy of the celestial realm.

Outside, the city was transformed into a magical spectacle. Lanterns and torches illuminated the streets, casting flickering shadows on the ancient walls. People danced and rejoiced, their movements reflecting the cyclical nature of life and the eternal dance between darkness and light.

The Festival of the New Moon was a time of joy and unity, when the people of Babylon came together to honor the celestial forces that governed their lives. It was a celebration of hope, a reminder that with each new moon, new possibilities emerged, and the divine favor was bestowed upon the city and its people.

As the night unfolded, the moon reached its zenith, casting a serene glow over the city of Babylon. The festival reached its crescendo, and the people offered their final prayers of gratitude and wishes for a prosperous future. They dispersed into the night, their spirits uplifted and hearts filled with the blessings of the new moon.

For generations to come, the Festival of the New Moon would remain a cherished tradition, a testament to the enduring connection between the people of Babylon and the celestial cycles that shaped their lives.

If this was performed today:

Preparation:

The city of Babylon comes alive with excitement and anticipation.

Merchants adorn their stalls with vibrant tapestries, exotic spices, and shimmering jewels.

Musicians practice their melodies, and performers rehearse their acts.

Babylonians from all walks of life gather in the central square, eager to partake in the festivities.

Gathering:

The High Priestess, dressed in flowing garments of celestial blue, leads the ceremonial procession towards the sacred temple.

The procession winds its way through the city streets, accompanied by dancers, musicians, and acrobats.

The crowd waves garlands of flowers and carries lit incense, symbolizing offerings to the moon goddess.

Invocation at the Temple:

The High Priestess ascends the grand staircase of the temple, radiating grace and reverence.

At the entrance, she raises her arms to the sky and invokes the blessings of the moon goddess, Ishtar.

She recites ancient prayers, calling upon Ishtar to shower her blessings upon the city and its inhabitants.

Sacred Rituals:

Inside the temple, the sacred fires burn bright, illuminating the altar adorned with offerings.

Offerings include ripe fruits, golden wheat, and sweet honey, symbolizing fertility, abundance, and prosperity.

The High Priestess and temple priestesses perform sacred rituals to honor the lunar energy and invoke its powers.

Chant and Hymns:

As the moon emerges in the night sky, the High Priestess leads the crowd in chants and hymns.

The rhythmic chorus reverberates through the temple, filling the space with the vibrancy of the celestial realm.

The chant/prayer might include invocations to Ishtar, praising her as the goddess of the moon and fertility, and seeking her blessings for the city and its people.

Celebration:

Outside the temple, the city is transformed into a magical spectacle.

Lanterns and torches illuminate the streets, creating a mesmerizing ambiance.

The people engage in joyful dancing and rejoicing, their movements reflecting the cyclical nature of life and the interplay between darkness and light.

Gratitude and Wishes:

As the moon reaches its zenith, the High Priestess guides the people in offering prayers of gratitude.

Individuals express their thanks for the blessings of the new moon and share their wishes for a prosperous future.

The prayers might include expressions of gratitude for the cyclical nature of life, the renewal brought by the new moon, and hopes for abundance and harmony.

Conclusion:

The festival reaches its crescendo, marking the culmination of the celebration.

The people disperse into the night, their spirits uplifted and hearts filled with the blessings of the new moon.

The Festival of the New Moon remains a cherished tradition, symbolizing the enduring connection between the people of Babylon and the celestial cycles that shape their lives.

Exploring Ancient Babylon's Rituals

The Rite of Passage for Warriors

As the sun dipped below the horizon, casting its golden glow upon the ancient city of Babylon, the time had come for the Rite of Passage for Warriors. The young warriors, adorned in gleaming armor and draped in vibrant ceremonial cloths, gathered in the courtyard of the training grounds. They stood tall, their hearts filled with anticipation and determination, ready to embark on this sacred journey of valor and honor.

Preparation:

The senior warriors, seasoned in battle and wisdom, led the preparations for the rite.

The ceremonial space was adorned with banners, bearing the symbols of strength and bravery.

The sacred fire, symbolizing the eternal flame of courage, burned brightly in the center of the courtyard.

Invocation and Blessing:

The High Priest, his voice resonating with solemnity, invoked the blessings of the gods of war and protection.

He offered prayers to Marduk, Ishtar, and Ninurta, beseeching their favor and guidance for the young warriors.

The warriors bowed their heads, receiving the blessings and strength bestowed upon them by the divine.

Ritual Cleansing:

The warriors approached a ceremonial basin filled with pure water, symbolizing the cleansing of the body and spirit.

They washed their hands, purifying themselves from the impurities of everyday life and embracing the purity of purpose.

The High Priest recited ancient incantations, calling upon the spirits of valor and protection to watch over the warriors.

Oath of Allegiance:

The warriors, one by one, stepped forward to recite the Oath of Allegiance, a solemn vow to protect the city, its people, and its sacred traditions.

They pledged their loyalty, dedicating their lives to defending the realm against any threat, whether foreign or domestic.

The High Priest, his voice unwavering, accepted their oath and bestowed upon them the sacred symbol of their warrior status.

Trial of Endurance:

The warriors were led to a designated arena, where they would face a series of physical and mental challenges.

The trials tested their strength, agility, strategic thinking, and ability to remain calm in the face of adversity.

The senior warriors and elders closely observed, evaluating the skills and character of each young warrior.

Communion with Ancestors:

After the trials, the warriors gathered in a sacred chamber adorned with ancestral relics and symbols.

They knelt before the ancestral shrine, honoring the spirits of their forefathers who had fought with valor before them.

The warriors sought the wisdom and guidance of their ancestors, connecting their spirits to the timeless lineage of warriors.

Celebration and Feasting:

As the night sky filled with stars, the warriors returned to the courtyard, triumphant and united.

A grand feast awaited them, a celebration of their initiation into the esteemed ranks of the warriors.

The city rejoiced, the sound of music and laughter filling the air, as the people honored their new protectors.

Reflection and Wisdom:

The warriors gathered once again, this time in a quiet chamber, illuminated by flickering torches.

The senior warriors imparted their wisdom, sharing tales of valor, resilience, and the importance of protecting the city's values.

The young warriors listened intently, their hearts filled with gratitude for the guidance of their mentors.

Blessing and Farewell:

The High Priest, his voice filled with pride, bestowed a final blessing upon the warriors.

He wished them courage, strength, and clarity of purpose as they embarked on their path of service.

The warriors embraced their loved ones, bidding farewell before embarking on their first missions as true defenders of Babylon.

The Rite of Passage for Warriors marked a significant milestone in the lives of these young Babylonian warriors. It was a sacred ceremony that honored their commitment to protect their city, upheld the values of honor and bravery, and forged a deep bond between warriors past and present. Through this rite, the warriors emerged as guardians of their people, ready to face the challenges of battle with unwavering resolve and unwavering loyalty to their sacred duty.

The Blessing of the Harvest

As the golden sun reached its zenith, casting a warm glow upon the fertile lands of Babylon, the people gathered to partake in the ancient rite known as the Blessing of the Harvest. The fields, adorned with ripened crops swaying in the gentle breeze, awaited the sacred invocation that would ensure abundance and prosperity for the coming season. The High Priest, adorned in ceremonial robes embroidered with symbols of growth and fertility, stood before the bountiful harvest, a symbol of life's sustenance.

Preparation:

The sacred site was prepared in the heart of the farmlands, adorned with colorful banners and bountiful offerings.

A beautifully crafted altar, adorned with sheaves of wheat, clusters of grapes, and other fruits of the land, stood at the center.

Invocation and Gratitude:

The High Priest, his voice resonating with reverence, called upon the gods of fertility and abundance.

The gathered farmers, their hands stained with the earth's rich soil, bowed their heads in gratitude and anticipation.

The High Priest offered a heartfelt prayer, expressing gratitude for the bountiful harvest and invoking the blessings of the gods upon the land.

Offering of First Fruits:

The farmers approached the altar, carrying baskets filled with the first fruits of the season's harvest.

They presented their offerings to the High Priest, who received them with solemnity and gratitude.

The High Priest placed each offering upon the altar, symbolizing the unity between the efforts of the farmers and the benevolence of the gods.

Chant of Abundance:

The High Priest led the gathered farmers in a chant, their voices rising in harmony, resonating with the rhythms of the earth.

The chant celebrated the cycle of life, the abundance of the land, and the eternal bond between humanity and the nurturing forces of nature.

The words of the chant carried the collective hopes and aspirations for a plentiful harvest and a prosperous future.

>(Chant)
>Oh, bountiful earth, giver of life,
>From your womb, abundance thrives.
>Fields of green and crops so fair,
>With gratitude, we offer our prayer.
>
>(Chorus)
>Abundance, oh, abundance,
>Flow upon our sacred land.
>By the gods' divine providence,
>May our harvest be grand.
>
>(Chant)
>Fertile soil, embrace each seed,
>Nourish and grow, fulfill our need.
>Sun's warm rays and gentle rain,
>Sustain the crops, remove all pain.
>
>(Chorus)
>Abundance, oh, abundance,
>Flow upon our sacred land.
>By the gods' divine providence,
>May our harvest be grand.
>
>(Chant)
>We toil with care, our labor true,
>In harmony with nature, we renew.
>As seasons turn, the cycle we trace,
>May prosperity adorn every space.

(Chorus)
Abundance, oh, abundance,
Flow upon our sacred land.
By the gods' divine providence,
May our harvest be grand.

(Chant)
With hearts sincere and voices strong,
We sing this chant, a grateful song.
By ancient bonds, we are connected,
In abundance, our souls protected.

(Chorus)
Abundance, oh, abundance,
Flow upon our sacred land.
By the gods' divine providence,
May our harvest be grand.

Blessing of the Fields:

The High Priest, holding a golden chalice filled with sacred water, moved through the fields, accompanied by the farmers.

He sprinkled the fields with the blessed water, invoking the gods to infuse the land with fertility and vitality.

As the water touched the earth, it was believed to awaken the dormant energies, ensuring the growth and abundance of the crops.

Communal Feast:

The Blessing of the Harvest culminated in a joyous communal feast, a celebration of gratitude and abundance.

The farmers and their families gathered around long tables laden with the harvest's bounty, sharing stories and laughter.

They offered portions of the blessed first fruits to the gods, expressing their appreciation for the blessings bestowed upon them.

Dance and Music:

The festivities continued with vibrant dances and melodic music that filled the air, accompanied by the rhythmic beat of drums and the trilling of flutes.

The people, young and old, swayed to the music, their movements reflecting the joy and vitality of the harvest season.

The dances and music were believed to honor the spirits of the land and express the collective gratitude of the community.

Through the Blessing of the Harvest, the people of Babylon sought to honor the divine forces that nurtured and sustained their lives. It was a time of gratitude, unity, and hope, a moment when the earthly and the divine intertwined, ensuring the continued abundance of the land and the prosperity of the people.

The Anointing of the Divine Kings

In the ancient city of Babylon, the Anointing of the Divine Kings was a sacred ceremony that symbolized the divine authority bestowed upon the chosen ruler. It was a momentous occasion, filled with grandeur and reverence, as the divine king received the blessings of the gods and was anointed with sacred oils.

The ceremony took place within the hallowed halls of the temple, adorned with intricate carvings and shimmering tapestries that depicted the ancient deities. The air was thick with incense, filling the space with a fragrant aroma, as the priests and priestesses prepared for the sacred ritual.

At the appointed time, the divine king, dressed in regal attire befitting his sacred role, entered the temple accompanied by a retinue of loyal attendants. The High Priest, adorned in ceremonial vestments, stood before the altar, holding a golden vessel filled with precious anointing oils.

The High Priest began the ceremony by invoking the blessings of the gods, reciting ancient prayers and invocations that bridged the mortal realm with the divine. The gathered congregation, consisting of priests, dignitaries, and loyal subjects, chanted sacred hymns that reverberated through the temple, their voices blending with the mystical energy of the moment.

With solemn grace, the High Priest approached the divine king, holding the golden vessel of anointing oil. Using a ceremonial brush made from sacred materials, the High Priest gently applied the consecrated oil to the forehead, shoulders, and hands of the divine king. Each stroke carried the symbolic significance of divine favor and protection.

As the anointing took place, the gathered congregation raised their hands in a gesture of reverence, their eyes fixed upon the anointed king. The air seemed to hum with an otherworldly energy, as if the gods themselves were present, bestowing their blessings upon the chosen ruler.

Throughout the anointing ceremony, prayers and invocations were recited, acknowledging the divine lineage of the king and beseeching the gods to guide and protect him during his reign. The anointing process was accompanied by the soft melodies of ancient instruments, their ethereal notes adding to the sacred ambiance of the moment.

Upon completion of the anointing, the High Priest pronounced the divine king as the chosen vessel of the gods' authority, their representative on Earth. The gathered congregation erupted in cheers and applause, their voices filling the temple with jubilation and celebration.

From that moment forward, the anointed king assumed his role with a heightened sense of purpose and responsibility. He was regarded as the embodiment of divine favor, entrusted with the welfare and prosperity of the kingdom. The Anointing of the Divine Kings served as a powerful symbol of the sacred bond between the mortal and divine realms, solidifying the king's authority and cementing his connection to the gods.

If this was performed today:

Preparation:

Sacred Space: Choose a suitable location that holds significance and sacredness. It could be a specially adorned room or a designated outdoor area decorated with symbols of royalty and divinity.

Altar: Set up an altar at the center of the space, adorned with rich fabrics, golden ornaments, and sacred symbols representing kingship and the divine.

Anointing Oil: Prepare a special anointing oil using natural ingredients like olive oil and essential oils with fragrances symbolizing purity, wisdom, and divine favor.

Robes and Accessories: Obtain ceremonial robes, crowns, scepters, and other regal accessories to enhance the visual representation of the divine kingship.

Invitations and Participants: Invite individuals who will play the roles of the Divine Kings, as well as attendees who will witness and partake in the ritual. Ensure that they are prepared and willing to fully embrace the significance of the ceremony.

The Ritual:

Purification:
a. The Divine Kings and participants gather at the designated sacred space.
b. A ceremonial purification is performed using water and fragrant herbs, symbolizing spiritual cleansing and readiness for the divine anointing.

Invocation and Blessings:
a. The High Priest or Priestess leads the ritual, standing before the altar.

b. The High Priest or Priestess offers invocations and prayers to the gods, calling upon their presence and blessings to infuse the ritual with divine power and guidance.
c. Attendees join in chanting or singing hymns, invoking the divine presence.

Anointing:
a. The Divine Kings step forward, wearing their ceremonial robes, crowns, and other regalia.
b. The High Priest or Priestess takes the sacred anointing oil and blesses it, invoking the blessings of the gods.
c. The High Priest or Priestess anoints the Divine Kings by gently applying the consecrated oil to their foreheads, symbolizing the divine blessings and authority bestowed upon them.

Blessings and Oaths:
a. The Divine Kings kneel before the altar, humbly accepting their divine calling and the responsibilities that come with it.
b. The High Priest or Priestess offers blessings and words of guidance, acknowledging the divine connection and the purpose of their rule.
c. The Divine Kings pledge oaths of service, promising to govern with wisdom, justice, and compassion.

Celebration:
a. The participants and attendees rejoice in the anointing of the Divine Kings, expressing their joy through music, dance, and feasting.
b. Performers showcase traditional dances, music, and theatrical presentations celebrating the kings' divine roles.
c. A communal feast takes place, featuring dishes that symbolize abundance and prosperity, such as grains, fruits, and celebratory delicacies.

Throughout the entire ceremony, it is essential to create an atmosphere of reverence, spirituality, and connection to the ancient traditions of Babylon. The focus should be on embracing the divine aspects of leadership and the responsibilities that come with it, as well as fostering a sense of unity and communal support.

The Marriage Ceremony of the Gods

In the ancient city of Babylon, the Marriage Ceremony of the Gods was a grand and sacred occasion, celebrated with utmost reverence and splendor. The ritual brought together the divine deities in a symbolic union, signifying the harmony of cosmic forces and the blessings bestowed upon the mortal realm. The ceremony unfolded as follows:

Preparation:

Sacred Temple: The sacred temple, adorned with intricate carvings and embellishments, served as the ceremonial venue. It stood tall, radiating divine energy, and was meticulously prepared for the auspicious occasion.

Altar and Offerings: A magnificent altar was erected at the heart of the temple, adorned with lush flowers, fragrant herbs, and offerings symbolizing fertility, abundance, and union. Golden vessels filled with sacred oils and perfumes were also placed on the altar.

Sacred Attire: The priests and priestesses adorned themselves in garments of vibrant colors, intricately woven with celestial symbols and sacred motifs. Their attire exuded a sense of divine presence and purpose.

Ritual Implements: The priests and priestesses carried ritual implements, including censers filled with fragrant incense, ceremonial vessels, and sacred adornments.

The Ceremony:

Invocation and Prayers: The High Priest or High Priestess, the appointed leader of the ritual, commenced the ceremony by invoking the gods and goddesses, calling upon their divine presence and blessings. The gathering would join in the solemn prayers, their voices resonating throughout the temple.

Procession of Deities: Priests and priestesses, representing various gods and goddesses, processed into the temple, bearing their respective symbols and attributes. Each deity's presence was announced, and the crowd greeted them with reverence and awe.

Sacred Union: The central moment of the ceremony was the symbolic union of the gods and goddesses. The High Priest or High Priestess led the ritual, uniting the divine couples in a sacred dance or ritual gesture, symbolizing the merging of cosmic forces and the harmony between male and female energies.

Blessings and Invocations: As the union of the gods and goddesses was celebrated, the High Priest or High Priestess offered prayers and invocations, beseeching the divine couple to bestow their blessings upon the mortal realm. They acknowledged the gods' eternal love and their roles as custodians of creation and fertility.

Ritual Offerings: The priests and priestesses approached the altar, presenting offerings of fruits, grains, and other sacred items to symbolize abundance, fertility, and prosperity. They poured libations of sacred oils and perfumes onto the altar, creating a fragrant and mystical atmosphere.

Sacred Hymns and Music: Musicians and singers filled the temple with enchanting melodies and harmonies, praising the divine couple and evoking a sense of transcendent joy. The crowd joined in the sacred hymns, their voices intertwining with the celestial sounds.

Divine Benediction: The High Priest or High Priestess, acting as the intermediary between mortals and deities, pronounced a benediction, bestowing the blessings of love, prosperity, and harmony upon the gathered assembly and the world beyond.

Festivities and Celebrations: Following the conclusion of the ceremony, the people of Babylon engaged in joyous celebrations, including feasts, dances, music, and theatrical performances. The entire city exuded an atmosphere of jubilation and unity, reflecting the divine union witnessed in the sacred ceremony.

The Marriage Ceremony of the Gods was a profound testament to the interconnectedness between mortals and deities, as well as the recognition of love, harmony, and the eternal cycle of creation. It served as a powerful reminder of the divine presence within and around every individual, fostering a sense of spiritual connection and reverence for the gods and goddesses who guided the destinies of both gods and mortals alike.

Here's a comparison between the ancient Babylonian Marriage Ceremony of the Gods and contemporary marriage ceremonies:

Purpose:

Ancient Babylon: The Marriage Ceremony of the Gods symbolized the union of divine forces and the blessings they bestowed upon the mortal realm.

Today: Modern marriage ceremonies typically celebrate the union of two individuals in love, creating a legal and emotional bond recognized by society.

Participants:

Ancient Babylon: The ceremony involved priests and priestesses representing various gods and goddesses, as well as the High Priest or High Priestess leading the ritual.

Today: Modern ceremonies involve the couple getting married, an officiant who conducts the ceremony, and often close family members and friends as witnesses.

Venue and Setting:

Ancient Babylon: The ceremony took place in a sacred temple adorned with elaborate decorations and altars.

Today: Modern ceremonies can be held in various locations such as religious buildings, outdoor settings, or event venues, reflecting the couple's preferences and cultural traditions.

Rituals and Symbols:

Ancient Babylon: The ceremony included invocations, prayers, sacred dances, and offerings symbolizing fertility, abundance, and union. The focus was on the divine union and cosmic harmony.

Today: Contemporary ceremonies often involve exchanging vows and rings as symbols of commitment and love. Additional rituals like lighting unity candles or pouring sand may be incorporated, reflecting personal beliefs or cultural customs.

Music and Celebrations:

Ancient Babylon: Musicians and singers filled the temple with sacred hymns, and festivities such as feasting, dancing, and theatrical performances followed the ceremony.

Today: Modern ceremonies often include music, with couples choosing songs that hold special meaning to them. After the ceremony, receptions are held, featuring speeches, meals, dancing, and other forms of entertainment.

Legal and Social Aspects:

Ancient Babylon: The ancient ceremony was primarily symbolic and had no legal implications.

Today: Contemporary ceremonies often have legal significance, requiring the completion of marriage licenses and registration. They also serve as a public declaration of commitment and are socially recognized.

While there are notable differences between ancient Babylonian Marriage Ceremonies of the Gods and modern marriage ceremonies, both share the common theme of union, love, and the celebration of a significant milestone in the lives of those involved.

Exploring Ancient Babylon's Rituals

Chapter 2
Incantations:

Exploring Ancient Babylon's Rituals

Incantation of Protection Against Evil Spirits

By the celestial powers that govern the realms,
By the ancient wisdom of the gods,
I call upon the forces of light and purity,
To shield us from the malevolent spirits that roam.

Oh, great Ishtar, goddess of love and war,
With your divine strength and fiery ardor,
Wrap us in your protective embrace,
And guard us against the darkness we face.

Mighty Marduk, master of the celestial domain,
Brandish your divine weapon and strike down the profane,
Banish the evil forces that seek to harm,
And keep us safe from all spiritual alarm.

I summon the spirits of the ancestors wise,
Those who have traversed the earthly skies,
Guide us with your wisdom, ancient and true,
Shield us from the malefic spirits that pursue.

I invoke the power of the sacred symbols and signs,
Etched upon amulets and sacred shrines,
With their divine presence, evil shall be undone,
And the purity of our souls shall brightly shun.

From the four corners of the earth, I summon protection,
The guardians of the elements in all their perfection,
Water, earth, fire, and air unite,
To repel the darkness with unyielding might.

By the sacred words and invocations profound,
I ward off evil, its whispers and its sound,
With divine light, we shall be illuminated,
Shielded from malevolence, we stand emancipated.

By the power of the gods and the cosmic decree,
I invoke this incantation, the key to set us free,
May the protective veil be cast around us all,
And evil spirits be banished, unable to befall.

In this ancient Babylonian chant of might,
We fortify our spirits, shining forth like a light,
Protected and secure, we walk on our path,
Shielded from evil, with hearts steadfast.

Let the incantation resonate, strong and clear,
Protecting us from harm, dispelling all fear,
Evil spirits, begone! By the gods, we are shielded,
In the embrace of divine protection, we are yielded.

In the ancient ways, we find solace and might,
Against the forces of darkness, we shall fight,
Protected and guided, we reclaim our power,
With this incantation, evil spirits shall cower.

So be it, as it was in the days of old,
By the words spoken and the spirits bold,
We invoke protection, our souls shall thrive,
Under the watchful gaze of gods, we shall survive.

Incantation to Invoke the Power of the Sun

Radiant Sun, majestic and divine,
I call upon your power to brightly shine.
With each dawn, your golden rays unfurl,
Illuminate our path and light the world.

Oh, Shamash, glorious god of the sun,
In your brilliance, our hopes are won.
From the eastern horizon, you arise,
Dispelling darkness with your radiant guise.

With each step, you traverse the sky,
Guiding us with your watchful eye.
Your warmth and light bring life anew,
Awakening the earth with colors and dew.

I invoke your power, oh Sun god bright,
To infuse us with your celestial light.
Grant us strength, vitality, and grace,
As we navigate life's intricate embrace.

As you journey across the heavenly dome,
Bless us with blessings from your eternal home.
Infuse our souls with your vibrant fire,
Ignite our passions and our hearts inspire.

Oh, Sun, source of life, so pure and true,
Illuminate our path with your fiery hue.
Bring us clarity, wisdom, and insight,
As we bask in your resplendent light.

By the ancient ways and sacred decree,
I call upon your power to set us free.
With each invocation, your energy aligns,
Empowering us as we traverse life's designs.

Oh, Shamash, hear our earnest plea,
Bestow your blessings upon you and me.
Fill our days with warmth and cheer,
As we walk in your presence, without fear.

In this incantation, your power I invoke,
To banish darkness and illuminate the yoke.
With your radiant essence, our spirits soar,
Embracing the vitality that you restore.

So, I beckon thee, oh Sun god divine,
To shine upon us and let your radiance shine.
In this sacred moment, our souls are one,
United with your brilliance, until time is done.

Incantation for Prosperity and Abundance

Oh, Marduk, mighty god of prosperity and abundance,
I call upon your divine presence, my heart you entrance.
With your benevolent power, bring wealth and success,
Let prosperity and abundance, upon me, impress.

From the depths of Eridu, your blessings flow,
As the Tigris and Euphrates rivers continuously grow.
Grant me fortune and riches, beyond measure,
Fill my life with abundance and endless treasure.

Oh, Nabu, god of wisdom and knowledge divine,
Bestow upon me your insight and mind so fine.
Guide my steps towards success and prosperity,
As I navigate life's path with clarity and sincerity.

By the sacred laws of Ishtar, goddess of love and fertility,
May blessings of abundance shower upon me, effortlessly.
Let my fields be fruitful, my harvest bountiful and grand,
As I prosper in all endeavors, guided by your hand.

I call upon Shamash, radiant god of the sun,
To illuminate my path and ensure victories won.
With your light and warmth, my fortunes enhance,
Bring forth prosperity, in every circumstance.

Let the gates of Babylon open wide,
As I attract wealth and abundance with unwavering stride.
May my business prosper, my ventures thrive,
As I embrace the blessings that abundantly arrive.

Oh, Anu, king of the gods, hear my plea,
As I invoke your divine presence, so free.
Grant me the favor of the heavens above,
And shower upon me prosperity and love.

By the ancient rites and sacred decree,
I claim prosperity and abundance for me.
May my days be filled with fortune's embrace,
As I live a life of abundance and grace.

In this sacred incantation, my intentions are clear,
To invite prosperity and abundance, without fear.
With gratitude and reverence, I embrace the divine,
And manifest a life of prosperity, truly sublime.

So, let it be, as I speak these words true,
May prosperity and abundance in my life accrue.
With the blessings of the gods, my fortune's restore,
And bring forth abundance forevermore.

Incantation for Love and Attraction

Oh, Ishtar, goddess of love and beauty divine,
I beseech you now, let your power intertwine.
With your captivating allure and magnetic grace,
Bring forth love's embrace in this sacred space.

By the banks of the Euphrates, where your temple stands,
I call upon your favor, reaching out my hands.
Fill my heart with the passion of your sacred fire,
Ignite the flames of love's desire.

Let your presence be felt in every word and deed,
As I attract a love that fulfills my every need.
May my aura radiate with irresistible charm,
Drawing love's enchantment, gentle and warm.

By the ancient laws of love and fate,
I invoke your blessings, dear Ishtar, great.
Guide me to the one whose soul aligns with mine,
Together we'll intertwine, an eternal love we'll find.

Oh, Shamash, god of radiant light,
Illuminate my path, make my love shine bright.
Bring forth connections, deep and true,
As I manifest a love that's pure and blue.

By the cosmic dance of the stars above,
I summon love's magic, boundless and of.
May my heart resonate with love's sweet song,
Attracting a love that will forever belong.

Oh, divine Anu, ruler of the celestial sphere,
Bless my love life, make it abundantly clear.
Grant me the joy and happiness I seek,
In love's embrace, may my spirit peak.

By the sacred laws of love's ancient decree,
I invite love's blissful energy to envelop me.
Open my heart, make it a vessel of love,
As I call forth a soulmate from the realms above.

With gratitude and reverence, I trust in your might,
To bring love's fulfillment, shining so bright.
May love's enchantment be forever mine,
As I speak this incantation, bound by the divine.

So mote it be, as I speak these words of power,
May love's sweet fragrance bloom like a flower.
I embrace the love that the universe will send,
And so it is, love's journey shall never end.

Incantation to Ward Off Disease and Illness

Oh, Ninurta, mighty god of healing and strength,
I beseech you now, hear my plea at length.
With your divine power and celestial might,
Protect me from illness, keep me safe day and night.

By the sacred rivers that flow through Babylon's land,
I call upon your aid, extending my hand.
Drive away sickness, banish it with your might,
Grant me health and vitality, shining so bright.

Oh, great Marduk, god of wisdom and grace,
I invoke your presence, may illness find no place.
With your guidance and wisdom, I seek your aid,
Shield me from harm, let no illness invade.

By the stars that twinkle in the midnight sky,
I summon your protection, as the illness tries.
Cleanse my body, purify my soul,
Grant me strength and wellness, make me whole.

Oh, Ea, god of medicine and wisdom untold,
I turn to you for healing, as the illness takes hold.
With your divine knowledge and skillful hand,
I trust in your guidance, let illness be banned.

By the ancient remedies and herbal lore,
I seek your intercession, let me be restored.
Cleanse my body, restore its balance and harmony,
Free me from disease, set my spirit free.

Oh, Ishtar, goddess of life and renewal,
I implore you now, make my body strong and dual.
Wrap me in your protective embrace,
Keep illness at bay, in every time and space.

By the chants of healers and the prayers of old,
I invoke your blessings, may illness unfold.
Fill me with vitality, from head to toe,
With your grace and favor, let wellness flow.

Oh, Shamash, god of light and warmth divine,
Illuminate my path, let my health always shine.
Protect me from illness, shield me from harm,
With your radiant energy, keep me strong and calm.

By the ancient rituals and sacred rites,
I ward off disease with all my might.
With every breath, I cleanse and purify,
Banishing illness, letting it pass me by.

So mote it be, as I speak these words of power,
May health and wellness blossom like a flower.
I am shielded from disease, in body and mind,
Under the divine protection, I am forever enshrined.

As it was in Babylon's ancient days of yore,
May this incantation guard me forevermore.
With gratitude and trust in your ancient ways,
I embrace your blessings, throughout my days.

Incantation to Control the Elements

By the powers of the ancient Babylonian realm,
I call upon the forces that govern the elements' helm.
With reverence and respect, I seek your command,
To control the winds, waters, earth, and fire, hand in hand.

Oh, mighty Marduk, lord of the skies so vast,
Grant me the power to control the winds that blast.
With a wave of my hand and a spoken decree,
Let the gusts obey, bending to my will, so free.

By the roaring rivers that flow through Babylon's heart,
I invoke their currents, to me they shall impart.
With a whispered word and a beckoning glance,
Let the waters flow under my control's advance.

Oh, Enki, god of the earth, fertile and rich,
Grant me dominion over the soil's every pitch.
With a firm step and a touch of my hand,
Let the earth respond, obeying my command.

By the flames that dance in the temple's sacred fire,
I call upon their essence, fueled by my desire.
With a focused gaze and a commanding voice,
Let the flames rise and fall, obedient to my choice.

Oh, Nergal, god of destruction and rebirth,
Grant me the power to control the elements' mirth.
With a steady mind and a heart filled with might,
Let the elements yield to my command, day and night.

By the ancient rituals and incantations of old,
I invoke the forces that the universe does hold.
Grant me the wisdom and the strength to master,
The elements' raw power, flowing faster and faster.

With respect and caution, I wield this gift divine,
Knowing that the balance must always align.
I control the elements with love and care,
Guided by ancient wisdom, aware and fair.

So mote it be, as I speak these words of might,
May the elements heed my call, day and night.
With their power under my command,
I harmonize with the cosmos, united, hand in hand.

Incantation to Invoke the Wisdom of the Gods

Oh, ancient gods of wisdom, hear my plea,
Grant me the knowledge that sets my spirit free.
From the celestial realms where your wisdom resides,
Bestow upon me the insights that wisdom provides.

Enki, god of wisdom and divine intellect,
Fill my mind with knowledge, I humbly reflect.
From the depths of your wisdom, I seek to learn,
Grant me the discernment, let my thoughts discern.

Marduk, god of justice and cosmic order,
Guide my path with wisdom, let me walk bolder.
Illuminate my path with your divine light,
So I may understand with clarity and insight.

Ishtar, goddess of love and divine beauty,
Infuse my heart with wisdom, pure and mighty.
Let me see the world with compassion and grace,
And share wisdom's blessings with all I embrace.

Nabu, god of writing and sacred words,
Empower my voice with the wisdom of the herds.
Grant me the eloquence to speak truth and inspire,
And let my words spread wisdom, higher and higher.

With reverence and respect, I invoke your names,
Oh, wise gods of old, with eternal flames.
Grant me the wisdom that your presence brings,
To navigate life's challenges, as wisdom sings.

From the depths of my soul, this incantation I send,
To invoke your wisdom, my eternal friends.
Fill my being with knowledge, ancient and true,
And guide me on a path where wisdom shines through.

So mote it be, as I speak with heartfelt devotion,
May the wisdom of the gods flow in endless motion.
I am open to receive your divine insight,
As I walk the path of wisdom, day and night.

Incantation for Clarity of Thought

Oh, ancient spirits of wisdom and insight,
I beseech you to lend me your guiding light.
In the realm of thought, I seek clarity,
To unravel the mysteries and see clearly.

By the power of the heavens above,
I invoke your aid with reverence and love.
Grant me a mind that's sharp and clear,
Free from confusion, doubt, and fear.

With each word spoken, each line I recite,
Let clarity of thought shine forth like a light.
Remove the fog that clouds my mind,
And let wisdom and understanding unwind.

Oh, ancient ones, bestow upon me,
The gift of discernment, so I may see.
Grant me focus, concentration, and insight,
To perceive the truth, both day and night.

As I chant these words with utmost devotion,
May my thoughts be filled with pure emotion.
Banish the distractions that hinder my way,
And guide me towards clarity every day.

With each breath I take, my mind aligns,
With the cosmic forces, the celestial signs.
Grant me clarity, so my thoughts may flow,
In harmony with the universe's eternal glow.

By the power of ancient knowledge and lore,
I seek clarity of thought forevermore.
As I speak this incantation with respect,
May my mind be sharp, intellect intact.

So mote it be, as I will it to be,
Clarity of thought, come forth to me.
I am open and receptive to your grace,
May clarity guide me in every thought and pace.

Incantation for Dream Divination

Oh, dreams that weave the tapestry of the night,
Reveal to me your secrets, visions so bright.
Through the realm of slumber, where messages reside,
Unveil the hidden truths that within you hide.

Hear my plea, O realm of dreams and the unknown,
Guide me to the wisdom that needs to be shown.
As I close my eyes and drift into your embrace,
Grant me the clarity to interpret your grace.

By the power of the moon and stars above,
I call upon the dream realm, the source of love.
Let my dreams become a gateway to insight,
Where symbols and messages come to light.

As I enter the realm of dreams with intent,
May my mind be open and my spirit be bent.
To receive the visions and symbols profound,
That hold the answers and truths yet unfound.

Great Morpheus, guardian of the dream domain,
Unveil the secrets that within me remain.
Guide me through the realms of the subconscious deep,
Where prophecies and revelations silently keep.

Through the dreamscape, I seek understanding,
In the realm of slumber, I find knowledge expanding.
Let the symbols speak with clarity and precision,
Revealing the path that leads to my soul's mission.

As the night unfolds, and dreams come alive,
May the messages I receive help me thrive.
Grant me the wisdom to decipher the signs,
And reveal the truths that within me aligns.

With gratitude and reverence, I call upon thee,
Dreams of the night, let your wisdom set me free.
As I sleep and journey in the astral plane,
May the visions and insights forever remain.

So let it be, as I speak this incantation true,
Dreams, I invoke your power, I trust in you.
Bring forth the divination that my dreams contain,
And guide me on a path where wisdom shall reign.

Incantation for Banishing Bad Luck

Oh, misfortune and ill luck that surround,
I call upon powers that abound.
With this incantation, I bid you away,
Banished from my life, no longer to stay.

By the strength of ancient forces unseen,
I break the chains of bad luck's routine.
Through the power of words and intent,
I sever the ties that keep me bent.

From the depths of darkness, I rise,
With positive energy that never dies.
I invoke the spirits, ancient and wise,
To shield me from misfortune's guise.

By the power of the sun, shining bright,
I cast away shadows that cloud my sight.
With every word I speak and every thought I think,
I create a shield that evil shall sink.

I call upon the four winds to carry away,
All traces of bad luck, keeping darkness at bay.
Let the cleansing breeze sweep through my life,
Removing strife and welcoming good fortune rife.

As I speak this incantation with heart and soul,
I release the grip of bad luck's control.
No longer shall it linger, no longer shall it bind,
With this incantation, peace of mind I find.

By the sacred fire's purifying flame,
I banish bad luck, dispelling its claim.
Gone are the curses, the hexes, and woe,
I embrace the blessings that now freely flow.

With every word spoken, the spell is cast,
Bad luck be gone, dissolved in the past.
I claim my destiny, filled with joy and cheer,
Banishing bad luck, as I stand strong and clear.

So mote it be, as I speak with might,
I banish bad luck and welcome delight.
By the ancient powers that watch from above,
I break the chains and embrace fortune's love.

May good luck prevail in all that I do,
As I walk this path, my spirit renewed.
With this incantation, bad luck is no more,
I am free to thrive, my spirit to soar.

Incantation to Open the Gates of the Underworld

Oh, ancient spirits of the deep,
I call upon you from the underworld's keep.
With reverence and respect, I seek your aid,
To open the gates where shadows are laid.

Through the realms of darkness and gloom,
I summon the spirits that dwell in the tomb.
With this incantation, I beckon them near,
To reveal their wisdom and secrets so clear.

By the power of the moon, shining bright,
I invoke the spirits of the eternal night.
Open the gates and grant me passage through,
To commune with the ancient souls anew.

Oh, guardians of the underworld's door,
Hear my plea and heed my implore.
With this incantation, I hold the key,
To unlock the gates and set spirits free.

Let the veil between realms grow thin,
As I step into the realm where shadows begin.
Grant me passage to the sacred abyss,
Where secrets and knowledge forever exist.

With every word spoken and every breath taken,
I embrace the darkness, unafraid and unshaken.
Guide me through the depths, spirits of old,
As I seek wisdom and truths yet untold.

By the ancient powers that govern the night,
I call upon you to grant me insight.
Open the gates, let the veil be lifted,
And reveal the mysteries that lie within, gifted.

As I venture into the realm of the deceased,
I honor and respect, my intentions released.

Exploring Ancient Babylon's Rituals

May the spirits guide and protect me on this quest,
As I delve into the realm where the shadows rest.

So it is spoken, so it shall be done,
With this incantation, the journey has begun.
I walk with courage, my spirit held high,
As the gates of the underworld open nigh.

Note: It is important to approach any invocation or incantation with caution and respect. This should not be used without proper knowledge, understanding, and cultural context.

Incantation for Astral Projection

Oh, ancient spirits of the astral plane,
I call upon your power to free me from the mundane.
With this incantation, I seek to transcend,
To travel beyond this realm, my spirit unbend.

By the moon's gentle glow and the stars above,
I ask for guidance on this astral voyage I love.
Grant me the ability to leave my earthly shell,
To explore the realms where dreams and visions dwell.

Oh, astral guardians, hear my plea,
Unlock the door to the astral sea.
Grant me wings to soar and eyes to see,
As I navigate the vastness of eternity.

With focused mind and unwavering will,
I release myself from earthly ties until
I traverse the realms of pure energy,
Where the fabric of existence dances freely.

Through the veil of consciousness, I'll pass,
Into the astral realm, where time is but a glass.
Let my spirit soar like a celestial bird,
Exploring the mysteries that have long been unheard.

Guide me, guardians, through the astral sphere,
Protect me from any harm or fear.
Grant me insight, wisdom, and clarity,
As I journey through the realms of duality.

With each breath, I rise above the mundane,
Embracing the freedom that astral travel contains.
May my spirit be light, my vision be keen,
As I explore the astral realms unseen.

By the power of the cosmos and the universe vast,
I embark on this journey, free from the past.
Astral projection, I invoke thee this night,
Grant me the power to transcend with all my might.

Exploring Ancient Babylon's Rituals

Note: Astral projection is a practice that should be approached with caution and proper guidance. This should not be tried without proper knowledge, understanding, and caution.

Incantation for Protection During Travel

In the realm of journeys, near and far,
I call upon protective powers that are.
As I embark upon this path unknown,
I seek your shield, a protective zone.

By the ancient forces that guard and guide,
I summon protection to travel beside.
From the four corners of the earth and sky,
I invoke your presence as I pass by.

Oh, guardians of travel, hear my plea,
Surround me with your shield, set me free.
From danger, harm, and ill intent,
Keep me safe wherever my journey is sent.

With every step I take, may your presence be near,
Shielding me from all that I should fear.
Create a barrier, strong and secure,
That repels negativity and keeps me pure.

Bless my vessel, whether land, air, or sea,
Make it a haven of safety for me.
May the winds carry me with gentle grace,
And the road ahead be a secure embrace.

Protect me from accidents, mishaps, and strife,
Keep me guarded throughout my entire life.
Guide my path with divine intervention,
Shielding me from harm, with divine prevention.

By the powers of ancient wisdom and might,
I invoke protection both day and night.
Grant me safe travels, wherever I roam,
And bring me back to the place I call home.

With gratitude and reverence, I send this prayer,
Knowing that your protection is always there.
Thank you, guardians of travel, for your aid,
For keeping me safe on this journey I've made.

Exploring Ancient Babylon's Rituals

Incantation for Fertility and Reproduction

By the ancient powers that govern life's creation,
I call upon the forces of fertile elation.
With reverence and devotion, I seek your aid,
To bless this endeavor, a new life to be made.

Oh, spirits of fertility, hear my plea,
Unleash your abundance and grace upon me.
From the depths of nature's womb, I beseech,
Grant me the gift of life, as I reach.

With the rising of the moon and the sun's embrace,
I invoke your essence, your life-giving trace.
In the sacred union of body and soul,
Let fertility blossom and life's story unfold.

Infuse my being with vitality and strength,
So that the seed of life may take its length.
In the embrace of love, let conception ignite,
Nurture the flame, let it burn bright.

By the powers of creation, ancient and pure,
I invoke the energy that will endure.
Bless my body, fertile ground so grand,
Bring forth the miracle as life is planned.

May the rivers of life flow within me,
As I embody the essence of fertility.
Grant me the joy of motherhood or fatherhood,
To nurture and guide, as every parent should.

With gratitude and reverence, I offer this prayer,
Knowing that your blessings are beyond compare.
Thank you, spirits of fertility, for your grace,
For bestowing upon me the gift of life's embrace.

Note: The above incantation is for fictional purposes only and should not be used as a substitute for medical advice or assistance in matters of fertility and reproduction. It is important to consult with healthcare professionals and address any concerns or questions regarding fertility and reproductive health.

Incantation for Divination with Sacred Objects

By ancient wisdom and mystical decree,
I seek the secrets hidden, waiting to be seen.
With sacred objects held in my hands,
I commune with spirits in distant lands.

O sacred objects, vessels of insight,
Reveal to me the truth, shining bright.
Let divination's veil be gently lifted,
As I delve into the realms, ancient and gifted.

With crystal's clarity and mirror's gaze,
I peer beyond the veil, through the haze.
Through runes and symbols, patterns unfold,
The mysteries of the future, waiting to be told.

O ancient spirits, guides unseen,
I call upon your wisdom, serene.
Breathe life into these objects, old and revered,
Open my mind to the messages I've endeared.

Let the pendulum swing with purpose and grace,
Unveiling answers from time and space.
Through tarot cards' archaic art,
Guide my hands to the answers held in each part.

With scrying mirrors, reflections deep,
Reveal the visions that I seek.
Through smoke and fire, the sacred flame,
Illuminate the path, from whence I came.

By bones cast upon the sacred ground,
The spirits' voices can be found.
From tea leaves' patterns in the cup,
Unveil the future, lift the shroud up.

By these sacred objects, blessed and true,
I open the gateway to wisdom, through and through.
May the spirits guide my hands and heart,
As I embark on this divination art.

With reverence and respect, I now decree,
That the secrets of the universe reveal themselves to me.
In harmony with the sacred flow,
I trust in the messages that divination will bestow.

Incantation for Binding and Unbinding

In the shadows' depths where powers reside,
I call upon forces to be my guide.
By the ancient art of binding and unbinding,
I shape the destinies, interweaving and finding.

With incantations spoken, words of might,
I harness the energies, both dark and light.
By knot and thread, by seal and mark,
I bind what's desired or set free what's stark.

By this incantation, I command and decree,
To bind or unbind, as my will shall be.
With intention pure and hearts aligned,
I shape the forces, both subtle and defined.

By binding knot, I seal the pact,
Restraining what's harmful, holding it intact.
With cords intertwined, a web of might,
I secure what's desired, keeping it tight.

But in the realm of freedom's reign,
I unbind the chains, releasing the strain.
By words of power and gestures bold,
I set free what's held, no longer controlled.

With ancient wisdom and knowledge vast,
I navigate the realms, present and past.
By the sacred balance of dark and light,
I bind what's harmful, unbind what's right.

But heed this warning, for it is true,
Binding and unbinding must be used with virtue.
Respect the laws of cause and effect,
For the energies unleashed, we must reflect.

In harmony with the cosmic flow,
I weave the incantation, and so it shall go.
With reverence and care, this spell is cast,
Binding and unbinding, a power unsurpassed.

Exploring Ancient Babylon's Rituals

Note: The concept of binding and unbinding can vary in different spiritual practices, and it is important to approach such practices with caution and ethical considerations.

Incantation to Invoke the Power of the Moon

Oh, radiant moon, in your celestial splendor,
I call upon your power, pure and tender.
Goddess of the night, with your mystical glow,
Awaken the magic within, let it flow.

In the silvered sky, your crescent form,
I seek your wisdom, serene and warm.
Embrace me with your lunar might,
Guide me through the shadows of the night.

Moon, enchantress of dreams and desires,
I beseech your presence, light my fires.
Illuminate the path to hidden realms,
Where secrets lie and mystic wisdom overwhelms.

With every phase, your energy shifts and sways,
I harness your power, in your gentle rays.
Empower my intuition, let it soar high,
As I navigate the realms where dreams lie.

Oh, moon so radiant, grant me your grace,
Illuminate my path, each step I embrace.
With your celestial guidance, I find my way,
In the darkest hours, you lead the day.

Moon goddess, keeper of ancient lore,
I invoke your essence, forevermore.
Infuse me with your tranquil light,
As I dance beneath the starry night.

In this sacred incantation, I proclaim,
The moon's power and magic, I aim to reclaim.
By your divine energy, I am blessed,
As I honor you, moon, in all my quests.

Note: The moon holds significance in various belief systems, and it is important to approach any spiritual practice or incantation with mindfulness and cultural sensitivity.

Incantation for Breaking Curses

By the ancient forces that govern this land,
I call upon powers to lend me a helping hand.
With spirits of light and energies divine,
I break the curses that have entangled and confined.

From the depths of darkness, I rise above,
Unraveling the bindings, restoring love.
With words of power and intentions clear,
I sever the chains that held me in fear.

By the strength of my spirit, unwavering and strong,
I dissolve the hexes that have done me wrong.
With every syllable uttered, with every breath I take,
I shatter the curses, their hold I break.

Through the veil of shadows, I see the light,
Dispelling the darkness, reclaiming my right.
By the ancient wisdom that courses through my veins,
I banish the curses, releasing their chains.

With clarity of mind and purity of heart,
I sever the ties that sought to tear me apart.
I call upon the spirits, benevolent and true,
To undo the curses and renew what is due.

With gratitude and reverence, I honor this release,
Breaking the curses, finding inner peace.
May the blessings of freedom forever remain,
As I step into light, released from all pain.

Note: If you believe you are under the influence of a curse, it is recommended to seek guidance from a qualified spiritual practitioner or healer.

Incantation to Communicate with Spirits

By the ethereal realms that lie beyond our sight,
I call upon spirits to guide me through the night.
With reverence and respect, I seek your presence here,
Grant me the gift to communicate, to make your voices clear.

In the sacred space between worlds, I stand,
A vessel of light, extending my hand.
With words of power and intention pure,
I invite the spirits to draw near and endure.

From realms unseen, I beckon your embrace,
Speak to me through whispers, reveal your grace.
With open heart and open mind, I listen and receive,
Your wisdom, your guidance, I humbly perceive.

By the ancient knowledge that weaves through time,
I call upon spirits, both gentle and sublime.
Through the veil of dimensions, we merge as one,
Grant me the gift to converse, until the ritual is done.

With respect and gratitude, I honor your presence,
Guiding me through realms of ethereal essence.
May our connection be strong, our communication clear,
As I commune with spirits, free from doubt and fear.

Note: When attempting to communicate with spirits, it is important to approach the practice with respect, caution, and a genuine intention. It is recommended to seek guidance from experienced practitioners and to create a safe and protected space before attempting any spirit communication rituals.

Incantation for Banishing Negative Energies

By the ancient forces that govern the cosmic tide,
I call upon the power to banish negativity far and wide.
With words of strength and spirit's flame,
I cleanse this space and release all that brings shame.

Oh, mighty winds, carry away the dark,
Let negativity be silenced, no longer leave a mark.
With the fiery passion that burns within,
I banish all that's harmful, let the healing begin.

By the Earth's grounding energy, firm and strong,
I sweep away negativity, where it doesn't belong.
With each step and every touch of the ground,
I cleanse this space, creating harmony profound.

In the sacred waters, pure and clear,
I wash away negativity, removing all fear.
As the rivers flow, carrying away the strife,
I release all negative energies, embracing new life.

By the light of the celestial stars above,
I call upon their radiance, their divine love.
Illuminate this space with positivity and grace,
Banishing darkness, filling every corner with a sacred embrace.

With the power of my voice, commanding and true,
I declare the banishment of negativity through and through.
No longer shall it linger, no longer shall it stay,
I reclaim this space, as I cast negativity away.

By the forces of nature and the universal flow,
I banish negative energies, making them go.
With each word spoken, with each intention set,
I cleanse this space, ensuring only light is met.

As this incantation ends, may the air be clear,
May positivity reign, dispelling all fear.
Banished are the negative energies, expelled and gone,

In their place, love and light forever will dawn.

Note: When performing the incantation for banishing negative energies, it is essential to focus on your intention and visualize the negative energies being removed from the space or from within yourself. Use your voice with conviction and confidence to command the banishment. After the incantation, it is beneficial to smudge the area with sacred herbs or perform a cleansing ritual to further purify the space.

Incantation for Rebirth and Renewal

From ashes to flames, from darkness to light,
I seek the power of rebirth, through the infinite might.
In the cycles of life, I shed the old and worn,
Embracing transformation, a new essence is born.

Oh, ancient forces of creation and renewal,
Unleash your magic, make me whole and true.
With every breath, with every beat of my heart,
I embrace the rebirth, ready for a brand-new start.

As the phoenix rises from the ashes, I soar,
Reclaiming my power, forevermore.
In the crucible of change, I'm purified,
Emerging stronger, with renewed purpose inside.

Grant me the courage to let go of the past,
To release what no longer serves, break free at last.
Like the seeds that sprout from the fertile ground,
I grow and blossom, with potential profound.

I invoke the energy of the cosmic dance,
Where death and rebirth forever enhance.
Grant me the wisdom to learn from the old,
And the strength to embrace the future, bold.

With every sunrise, with every moon's glow,
I am reborn, with passion and purpose, I know.
In the eternal cycle of life's sacred embrace,
I welcome renewal, as I claim my rightful place.

By the powers of the universe, I affirm my worth,
I am reborn, a soul experiencing rebirth.
In this sacred moment, I embrace the divine,
Renewed, revitalized, forever intertwined.

Note: The incantation for rebirth and renewal is a personal and introspective practice. It is recommended to perform this ritual with sincere intent and a genuine desire for transformation. Embrace the energies of change and renewal, and allow yourself to let go of the past to make way for new beginnings.

Incantation to Invoke the Wisdom of the Ancestors

Oh, ancient spirits, wise and revered,
I call upon your guidance, so revered.
From the depths of time and beyond the veil,
I seek your wisdom, I humbly prevail.

Ancestors, mighty souls of old,
With knowledge and insight, your stories unfold.
In realms unseen, where mysteries reside,
I invoke your presence, by my side.

Through the whispers of time, your voices I hear,
In sacred stillness, your wisdom draws near.
From generation to generation, your legacy passed,
I embrace your teachings, steadfast.

Oh, ancestors, guardians of ancient lore,
Guide me on this path I explore.
Illuminate my mind with your sacred light,
Grant me wisdom and clarity, shining bright.

In the sacred chamber of my heart and soul,
I open the gateways, I make you whole.
Your ancient knowledge, deep and profound,
Fills me with understanding, all around.

By the blood that flows within my veins,
I honor your wisdom, free from chains.
With reverence and respect, I humbly plea,
Unveil the truths that are meant for me.

Ancestors, I seek your counsel divine,
In this sacred space, our spirits intertwine.
Grant me the wisdom, the insight I seek,
So I may walk my path, strong and meek.

By the power of our ancestral bond,
I receive your wisdom, eternal and beyond.

In gratitude and love, I offer my praise,
For your guidance and blessings, all my days.

Note: When performing the incantation to invoke the wisdom of the ancestors, create a peaceful and sacred space where you can connect with their energy. Light candles or incense, if desired, to create an atmosphere of reverence. Speak the incantation with sincerity and focus, allowing yourself to be open to receiving their guidance and wisdom. Trust in the connection you have with your ancestors and be receptive to the messages and insights they may provide.

Incantation for Safe Journey in the Afterlife

Oh, departed souls, on this sacred night,
I call upon your presence, shining bright.
Guide me through the realms beyond,
To the place where eternal peace is found.

As I embark on this journey of transition,
Grant me safe passage, free from affliction.
Protect my soul, O spirits of the divine,
As I traverse the realms, so sublime.

I call upon the guardians of the afterlife,
With reverence and respect, I seek your strife.
Wrap me in your ethereal embrace,
Shield me from darkness, in every space.

May my spirit soar, untouched by harm,
Through the boundless realms, with tranquil charm.
Navigate the paths with wisdom and grace,
As I journey to the eternal resting place.

Illuminate my way with your guiding light,
Guide me through the shadows of the night.
Protect me from malevolent forces that lurk,
As I tread the path, where spirits work.

Oh, ancient guardians, guardians of the soul,
In your presence, I feel truly whole.
Keep me safe, as I cross the divide,
To the realm where peace and serenity reside.

By the power of your watchful eyes,
May my journey be blessed, devoid of cries.
Lead me to the realms of eternal bliss,
Where my spirit finds solace, in your midst.

In the realm of the afterlife, I find my rest,
In your care, my soul is forever blessed.
I offer my gratitude, my humble plea,
For your protection and guidance, eternally.

Note: When performing the incantation for a safe journey in the afterlife, create a sacred space where you can connect with the spirits. Light candles or incense to honor the departed and create a serene atmosphere. Speak the incantation with sincerity and reverence, visualizing a safe and peaceful journey through the realms beyond. Trust in the guidance and protection of the guardians of the afterlife and believe in the power of the words spoken.

Incantation for Breaking Spiritual Attachments

By the ancient powers that dwell unseen,
I call upon your strength, radiant and keen.
Release the bonds that hold me tight,
Break these spiritual attachments with your might.

Spirits that cling and hold me bound,
I command you to depart, to no longer be found.
You have no power over me, I declare,
I sever these ties, now and forever I bear.

With the force of light and divine decree,
I banish your presence, set my spirit free.
From negative attachments, I am released,
In the sacred space of love and peace.

By the strength of my will and inner light,
I break the chains that bind, dispelling the night.
I reclaim my power, my sovereignty,
No longer burdened by your hold over me.

With every word spoken, every intention set,
I dissolve your presence, without regret.
I call upon the forces of love and grace,
To cleanse and heal, filling every space.

Spiritual attachments, now be gone,
I reclaim my spirit, resilient and strong.
I stand in my truth, protected and whole,
Breaking these bonds, restoring my soul.

With this incantation, I sever the ties,
Breaking free from all that corrupts and denies.
I walk the path of light and purity,
Released from all spiritual attachments, I decree.

Note: When performing the incantation for breaking spiritual attachments, create a sacred and protected space where you feel safe. Light candles or burn cleansing herbs to purify the energy. Speak the incantation with conviction and confidence, visualizing the spiritual attachments dissolving and fading away. Trust in the power of your intention and the support of divine forces as you release and let go. After the incantation, engage in self-care practices to nurture and strengthen your spirit.

Incantation for Protection of Sacred Spaces

By the ancient powers that guard and shield,
I call upon your strength, ancient and concealed.
Protect this sacred space, this hallowed ground,
With your divine presence, let safety be found.

From all negative forces, I create a ward,
Guarding this space with divine accord.
No harm shall enter, no ill shall prevail,
Only love and light within this sacred veil.

I invoke the guardians of ancient might,
To watch over this space, day and night.
Let no darkness taint its sanctity,
Only pure energies and tranquility.

With every word spoken and intention set,
I create a barrier that none can forget.
By the power of divine light and grace,
I secure this space, a sacred dwelling place.

No malevolent spirits shall dare to trespass,
Boundaries of protection, none can surpass.
This space is shielded, a sanctuary divine,
Where only positivity and blessings intertwine.

From corner to corner, from wall to wall,
I call upon the protective forces to install,
A shield of pure energy, strong and true,
Ensuring this space remains safe and true.

By the power of sacred words and ancient lore,
I seal this protection forevermore.
May this space be a haven of love and peace,
Shielded from harm, its blessings increase.

Note: When performing the incantation for the protection of sacred spaces, create a sacred atmosphere by cleansing the space with purifying herbs or incense. Visualize a radiant shield of light surrounding and permeating the space, providing a protective barrier. Speak the incantation with authority and belief, invoking the protective forces to safeguard the sacred space. Trust in the power of your intention and the assistance of higher energies as you establish and reinforce the protective barrier. Regularly renew and reinforce the protection to maintain the sanctity of the space.

Incantation for Communicating with Animal Spirits

Oh, spirits of the wild, ancient and wise,
I call upon you, with reverence in my eyes.
Grant me the gift of understanding deep,
To commune with animal spirits, their secrets to keep.

By the powers of nature and creatures divine,
I seek connection, a bridge I shall align.
Open the channels, let our spirits unite,
In the realm of the animal, share your insight.

Guide my steps on this sacred path,
Grant me the language to understand and ask.
With respect and love, I approach your realm,
To communicate with clarity, overwhelm.

By the wisdom of the animal kingdom vast,
I invite your presence, from present to past.
Teach me your ways, your ancient lore,
To learn and grow, forevermore.

Through the rustle of leaves, and whispering wind,
I seek your messages, where meanings begin.
Speak to me through signs, symbols, and sounds,
Reveal your teachings, profound and profound.

With reverence and gratitude, I honor your kind,
Your spirits entwined with nature's bind.
Guide me, protect me, as I walk this Earth,
In harmony with all creatures, celebrating their worth.

By the power of intention and heart sincere,
I connect with animal spirits, drawing near.
May our communication be pure and true,
As I learn from you, as you teach me too.

Note: When performing the incantation for communicating with animal spirits, find a quiet and natural setting where you can connect with the energy of the wild. Ground yourself and open your heart to the presence of animals. Speak the incantation with sincerity and respect, inviting the spirits of the animal kingdom to join you in communication. Observe the signs, symbols, and behaviors of animals as they may offer messages and insights. Trust your intuition and be open to receiving their wisdom and guidance. Remember to always approach wildlife with caution and respect, keeping a safe distance and not disturbing their natural habitats.

Incantation for Banishing Night Terrors

By the power of the moon, shining bright,
I banish night terrors, the frightful plight.
In the realm of dreams, I take my stand,
To ward off darkness with a guiding hand.

From the depths of fear, I set myself free,
No longer bound by what I cannot see.
With this incantation, I break the spell,
Night terrors flee, bidding them farewell.

Guardians of dreams, protect and guide,
Banish the shadows, where fears reside.
With each breath, I release the fear's hold,
Nightmares disperse, their power unfolds.

I call upon the light of divine grace,
To cleanse my dreams, creating sacred space.
Surround me with love, comfort, and peace,
As I slumber, let fear's grip cease.

In the realm of sleep, I claim my power,
To shape my dreams, each passing hour.
Nightmares vanish, replaced by delight,
A peaceful realm, where dreams take flight.

By the strength of my will and inner light,
I banish night terrors, they take their flight.
No longer bound by fear's dark grip,
I embrace restful slumber, a peaceful trip.

In dreams, I find serenity and calm,
No longer haunted by night's alarm.
With this incantation, I set myself free,
Night terrors banished, no longer decree.

Note: When performing the incantation for banishing night terrors, create a soothing and calming environment in your bedroom. Light candles or use a nightlight to create a gentle ambiance. Take deep breaths, allowing your body and mind to relax. Speak the incantation with confidence and belief, visualizing the fear and night terrors dissipating, leaving a space of peace and tranquility. Before sleep, engage in calming activities such as reading or listening to soothing music. Trust in the power of your intention and the support of divine forces as you banish night terrors and invite restful sleep.

Incantation for Divination with Sacred Numbers

In the realm of sacred numbers, I seek to divine,
Reveal the secrets hidden, with clarity and shine.
By the power of numerology, ancient and profound,
I call upon their guidance, their wisdom to astound.

Number one, the beginning, the spark of creation,
Grant me insight and inspiration, divine revelation.
Number two, the balance, the duality in sight,
Reveal the harmony and connections, shining bright.

Number three, the trinity, the union of mind, body, soul,
Unveil the deeper meanings, the insights to behold.
Number four, stability, the foundation and strength,
Guide me in grounding and manifesting, to great lengths.

Number five, the change, the adventure and surprise,
Show me new opportunities, where growth lies.
Number six, harmony, the nurturing and care,
Reveal the paths of love and abundance, everywhere.

Number seven, spirituality, the mystic and divine,
Open the gateways to wisdom, the secrets intertwined.
Number eight, abundance, the infinite flow,
Lead me to prosperity, where blessings bestow.

Number nine, completion, the end of a cycle,
Illuminate the lessons learned, with grace and style.
In the sacred language of numbers, I seek insight,
Divine the patterns and meanings, shining bright.

By the power of numerology, ancient and grand,
I open myself to the messages, as they expand.
Guide me, sacred numbers, in divination's embrace,
Reveal the hidden knowledge, with wisdom and grace.

Note: When performing the incantation for divination with sacred numbers, create a focused and tranquil environment where you can connect with the energy of the numbers. Take deep breaths and center yourself. Choose a specific number or set of numbers to focus on for your divination. Speak the incantation with clarity and intention, allowing the energy of the numbers to flow through you. Be open to receiving insights, symbols, or patterns that may emerge during your divination practice. Trust your intuition and the guidance of the sacred numbers as you explore their meanings and messages.

Incantation for Healing Emotional Wounds

In the depths of my being, I seek solace and release,
To heal the wounds within, and find a sense of peace.
By the power of ancient wisdom and divine love,
I call upon healing energies from realms above.

Oh, spirits of compassion, grace, and tender care,
Wrap me in your embrace, with healing light so rare.
With this incantation, I release all that no longer serves,
The burdens and the pain, let them dissolve and curve.

By the strength of my intention and the power of my will,
I reclaim my inner strength, my heart begins to heal.
I call upon the healing energies of earth, water, air, and fire,
To restore my balance, ignite the sacred healing pyre.

Gentle breeze, blow away the anguish and despair,
Cleanse my heart and mind, and fill them with repair.
Flowing waters, wash away the tears of sorrow and grief,
Nurture my wounded soul, bringing me relief.

Oh, sacred fire, burn away the scars and fears,
Transform them into courage, as the smoke disappears.
Earth beneath my feet, ground me in stability and calm,
Support my healing journey with your nurturing balm.

With every word I speak, with every breath I take,
I release the pain and hurt, and let my spirit awake.
I choose forgiveness and love, to mend what has been torn,
Embracing healing energies, as I am reborn.

May this incantation be a catalyst for transformation,
Healing emotional wounds with divine affirmation.
By the power of the ancients and the universe's embrace,
I am healed, I am whole, I walk in love and grace.

Note: This incantation is a personal invocation for healing emotional wounds. Perform this ritual in a quiet and sacred space where you can focus your energy. Speak the incantation with intention and sincerity, allowing its words to resonate within you. Visualize the healing energies enveloping your being, releasing emotional pain and fostering inner peace. Repeat this incantation as needed, allowing it to support your healing journey. Remember to seek professional help or guidance if you are dealing with deep emotional wounds or trauma.

Incantation for Amplifying Magical Intention

By the powers that be, both seen and unseen,
I call upon the forces to make my intention keen.
With focused mind and heart aligned,
I amplify my magic, with power combined.

From the depths of my being, I draw strength and will,
To manifest my desires, my intention to fulfill.
By the elements of earth, air, fire, and water,
I harness their energy, weaving the spell I ought to.

Oh, sacred earth, stable and strong,
Infuse my intention, carry it along.
Grant me the grounding to manifest my will,
As I channel your energy, my purpose to fulfill.

Mighty air, swift and free,
Carry my intentions on the winds, with glee.
Expand my magic, let it soar high,
To reach the realms where dreams reside.

Fiery flame, burn bright and true,
Ignite my intention, let it break through.
Transform all obstacles into ash and dust,
As my magic takes form, in you I trust.

Waters pure, flowing and deep,
Cleanse and purify, my intentions to keep.
Empower my magic with your fluid grace,
As I navigate the currents of time and space.

With every word spoken and gesture made,
I amplify my intention, like a serenade.
I align myself with the cosmic flow,
Let my magic radiate and glow.

As above, so below, as within, so without,
My intention takes shape, there is no doubt.
By the power of the universe, ancient and wise,
I amplify my magic, under celestial skies.

Note: This incantation is meant to amplify your magical intention. Perform it with respect and clarity of purpose, understanding that your intentions carry responsibility. Focus your mind and visualize your intention manifesting as you speak the incantation. Feel the energy of the elements supporting and amplifying your magic. Remember to always use your magic responsibly and in alignment with the highest good of all.

Incantation for Strengthening the Aura

In the realm of energies that surround,
I call upon the forces, profound.
With this incantation, I empower and align,
To strengthen my aura, a shield divine.

By the sacred elements, earth, air, fire, and sea,
I invoke their power, merging within me.
From the depths of the earth, stability I gain,
Grounding my aura, a firm and steady terrain.

In the swift currents of air, I find clarity and light,
Cleansing my aura, removing all that's not right.
I breathe in the winds, rejuvenating my core,
Expanding my aura, open to wisdom's door.

Through the flames of fire, passion ignites,
Infusing my aura, with courage and might.
I embrace the heat, burning away what's old,
Radiating my aura, a blaze of strength untold.

In the waters of the sea, emotions flow,
Healing my aura, with their soothing glow.
I dive deep within, cleansing and renewing,
Flowing through my aura, a gentle fluidity ensuing.

By the power of my intent, I claim my space,
Enveloped in light, my aura's grace.
A shield of protection, strong and pure,
Radiating from within, steadfast and sure.

Negative energies, they shall not pass,
My aura repels them, like a tempered glass.
With each breath I take, I strengthen my shield,
Empowering my aura, as my spirit is revealed.

May this incantation fortify my aura's embrace,
A luminous boundary, safeguarding my space.
With love and light, I stand in my power,
Radiating my aura, vibrant like a flower.

Note: This incantation is intended to strengthen and protect your aura. As you recite the incantation, visualize your aura expanding and becoming stronger, forming a protective shield around you. Feel the energy of the elements merging with your aura, empowering and cleansing it. Remember to regularly cleanse and maintain your aura through practices such as meditation, energy work, and self-care.

Incantation for Banishing Envy and Jealousy

In the realm of spirits, I now proclaim,
A sacred incantation to banish envy's flame.
From the depths of my being, I rise above,
Releasing all jealousy with grace and love.

By the power of light, I cleanse my soul,
Unraveling envy, making it lose control.
I call upon the spirits, wise and kind,
To aid me in freeing my heart and mind.

Envy, begone, from this sacred space,
No longer shall you dwell within, no trace.
I release the chains that bind my heart,
Replacing envy with gratitude, a brand new start.

I embrace the joy that others may find,
Their success and blessings, I celebrate in kind.
For I know that abundance is endless and vast,
There's enough for all, present and future, to last.

I let go of comparisons, of what others possess,
Focusing on my own path, with happiness I progress.
I honor my journey, unique and divine,
Embracing my gifts, allowing them to shine.

With this incantation, envy I dispel,
Creating space for love and peace to dwell.
I walk this world with an open heart,
Free from envy's grip, I make a fresh start.

By the ancient forces that guide my way,
I release envy's hold, starting today.
I choose love, compassion, and self-worth,
Banishing envy, embracing my own mirth.

So mote it be, let it be done,
Envy's power now dissolved and undone.
With this incantation, I reclaim my peace,

Free from envy's burden, my soul finds release.

Note: This incantation is intended to help release feelings of envy and jealousy and promote a sense of gratitude, contentment, and self-worth. As you recite the incantation, visualize the negative emotions of envy and jealousy leaving your being and being replaced by love, compassion, and gratitude. Focus on embracing your own unique path and celebrating the successes and blessings of others. Practice self-care and cultivate a mindset of abundance to further support your journey towards banishing envy and embracing positivity.

Incantation for Releasing Past Trauma

In the depths of time, where memories reside,
I call upon the forces, to heal and provide.
With this incantation, I release the past,
Freeing myself from trauma that no longer lasts.

From the shadows deep, where pain does reside,
I summon strength and courage to heal inside.
I call upon the spirits, ancient and wise,
To guide me through healing, where darkness lies.

With sacred words and intentions pure,
I sever the chains that trauma did endure.
I release the hold of past wounds and strife,
Embracing a future filled with joy and life.

By the power of love and divine grace,
I reclaim my essence, in a sacred space.
I let go of the pain, the hurt, and despair,
Opening my heart, allowing healing to repair.

I summon the strength to face what's been,
To heal the scars and let the light shine within.
I release the burden, the weight I no longer bear,
Transforming my wounds with tender care.

I embrace forgiveness, for myself and all,
Releasing resentment, answering the divine call.
I reclaim my power, my essence, my truth,
Rising above the past, renewing my youth.

With this incantation, I break the chains,
Setting myself free from past trauma's pains.
I step into the present, empowered and strong,
Creating a future where healing belongs.

So mote it be, let it be done,
The release of past trauma, a new chapter begun.
With this incantation, I reclaim my life,
Free from the grip of past trauma's strife.

Note: This incantation is intended to help release the emotional and energetic imprints of past trauma. As you recite the incantation, focus on letting go of the pain, hurt, and negative emotions associated with the trauma. Visualize the chains of the past breaking and dissolving, allowing healing and renewal to take place. Practice self-care, seek support from loved ones or professionals, and engage in healing practices that resonate with you to further support your journey of releasing past trauma.

Incantation for Empowering Talismans

By the ancient forces that weave the web,
I empower this talisman, a sacred eb.
With the power of the elements, I bestow,
An enchantment of strength, wherever it may go.

From earth's firm foundation, stability it gains,
Grounding its energy, as it remains.
From air's gentle whispers, clarity it receives,
Guiding its purpose, as it perceives.

From fire's fierce blaze, passion it ignites,
Fueling its essence, as it takes flight.
From water's flowing grace, emotions it flows,
Cleansing its spirit, as it knows.

With this incantation, I charge this charm,
Infusing it with power, safe from harm.
May it radiate protection, courage, and might,
Empowering its wearer, both day and night.

By the strength of the sun, its brilliance and heat,
I awaken its potential, making it complete.
By the light of the moon, its mystical glow,
I bless it with wisdom, as it continues to grow.

With every word spoken, intentions align,
Harnessing the energies, both yours and mine.
Together we empower this talisman true,
Amplifying its energy, as it serves you.

As it adorns your person, or rests in your hand,
Feel its power radiate, as it takes a stand.
May it shield you from darkness, and negativity's sway,
Guiding you on your path, each and every day.

So mote it be, let it be done,
Empowered by the moon, and the golden sun.
With this incantation, the talisman is blessed,
Carrying the energy, of power manifest.

Note: This incantation is meant to charge and empower a talisman with specific intentions, such as protection, courage, or any other desired quality. As you recite the incantation, visualize the energy flowing into the talisman, infusing it with the intended power. Feel the connection between yourself, the energies of the elements, and the talisman. Carry or wear the talisman with confidence, knowing that it holds the empowered energy you have invoked.

Incantation for Blessing Sacred Jewelry

By the ancient forces that weave through time,
I call upon the divine in this sacred rhyme.
With reverence and respect, I gather near,
To bless this jewelry, holding blessings dear.

Oh, sacred jewelry of precious design,
Carrying symbolism, ancient and divine.
Through the hands that crafted you, I see,
The beauty and power you hold within thee.

With every gem and metal, so carefully set,
I bless this jewelry, with a sacred debt.
May it radiate love, harmony, and grace,
Enhancing the wearer's sacred space.

In the presence of the moon and shining sun,
I invoke their energies, intertwining as one.
Moon, bless this jewelry with your gentle light,
Infusing it with intuition, guidance, and sight.

Sun, bless this jewelry with your fiery might,
Igniting passion, courage, and inner light.
Let it shine brightly, reflecting your rays,
Empowering the wearer throughout their days.

I call upon the Earth, ancient and wise,
To bless this jewelry, grounding its ties.
May it connect to the nurturing embrace,
Providing strength and balance in every place.

Air, bring clarity and wisdom to this adornment,
Clearing the mind, fostering enlightenment.
Let it carry the whispers of inspiration and thought,
Guiding the wearer in the wisdom they sought.

Water, bless this jewelry with emotions pure,
Cleansing and healing, offering solace and cure.
May it carry the essence of love and compassion,
Bringing comfort and soothing any inner tension.

With this incantation, I infuse this jewelry with light,
Aligning it with the energies both day and night.
May it serve as a reminder of sacred connection,
A talisman of blessings, a symbol of protection.

As it adorns the wearer, it carries this decree,
To bring blessings, joy, and harmony, so mote it be.
With gratitude and reverence, this blessing I impart,
May this jewelry bring blessings to the wearer's heart.

Note: When performing this incantation, hold the sacred jewelry in your hands and visualize it being bathed in the energies of the elements as you recite the words. Imagine the jewelry becoming infused with the qualities and blessings associated with each element mentioned. Feel the connection between the jewelry, the elements, and the intention you are setting. Carry or wear the jewelry with gratitude and awareness of the blessings it carries.

Incantation for Banishing Negative Thoughts

In the realm of mind, where thoughts do dwell,
I call upon the power within me to dispel.
Negative thoughts that linger and persist,
I banish you now, no longer to exist.

By the strength of my will and the light within,
I release negativity, let new beginnings begin.
From the depths of my being, I rise above,
Shedding the weight, embracing self-love.

I summon the forces of clarity and peace,
To cleanse my mind and grant release.
With this incantation, I break the chains,
Freeing my thoughts from negative domains.

No longer shall doubts and fears hold sway,
Positive vibrations shall light my way.
I release the grip of negativity's hold,
Embracing thoughts that are empowering and bold.

By the power of the elements, I declare,
I am the master of my thoughts, aware.
I banish the darkness, let light shine through,
Transforming negativity into something new.

As the winds of change blow through my mind,
I embrace positivity of every kind.
With each breath, I release what no longer serves,
Inviting in thoughts that uplift and preserve.

With this incantation, I declare my intent,
To banish negative thoughts, their energy spent.
I am the sovereign of my mental space,
Filling it with thoughts of love and grace.

By the ancient wisdom that guides us all,
I banish negative thoughts, big and small.
From this moment forward, my mind is clear,
Filled with positivity, free from any fear.

So mote it be, as I speak this decree,
Negative thoughts, now I set you free.
I claim my power, my thoughts I control,
Banishing negativity, restoring my soul.

Note: As you recite this incantation, envision negative thoughts dissolving and being replaced by positive, uplifting thoughts. Feel a sense of clarity and lightness in your mind as you release the negative energy. Embrace the power of your intention to banish negative thoughts and affirm your ability to cultivate positivity and peace within your mind. Repeat this incantation as often as needed to reinforce your commitment to banishing negative thoughts and maintaining a positive mindset.

Incantation for Awakening Inner Power

In the depths of my being, a power resides,
Awakening now, as the tides.
I call forth the strength that lies within,
To rise and flourish, let my journey begin.

I summon the fire that burns deep inside,
Igniting my passion, my power, my stride.
From the embers, I rise with might,
Unleashing my potential, shining bright.

With every breath, I claim my space,
Awakening my inner power, embracing grace.
I shed the doubts that held me back,
Unlocking my potential, staying on track.

I am the creator of my own destiny,
Harnessing the power that flows through me.
With focused intent, my energy aligns,
Awakening my power, transcending confines.

I call upon the Earth, stable and strong,
Grounding my power, where I belong.
From the depths below, strength does arise,
An unwavering force, a limitless prize.

I invoke the air, the winds that inspire,
Fanning the flames of my inner fire.
With clarity and wisdom, I soar high,
Embracing my power, reaching the sky.

I draw upon the water, fluid and free,
Nurturing my spirit, setting my power free.
Emotional depths, intuition untold,
Awakening my power, a force to behold.

I connect with the ether, the boundless space,
Tapping into cosmic energy's embrace.
Transcending limitations, expanding my mind,
Awakening my power, the infinite I find.

By the ancient forces that guide my way,
I awaken my inner power, day by day.
I claim my birthright, my strength untold,
Embracing my power, I now unfold.

With this incantation, I set myself free,
Awakening my power, I choose to be.
I step into my purpose, with confidence and might,
Unleashing my potential, shining ever bright.

So mote it be, as I speak this decree,
Awakening my power, so mote it be.
I embrace my true self, bold and true,
Awakening my inner power, I am anew.

Note: As you recite this incantation, visualize yourself tapping into the dormant power within you. Feel the energy awakening and flowing through your body, empowering you from within. Embrace the elements and their respective qualities as you invoke them, feeling their presence and support in awakening your inner power. Affirm your intention to embrace your true self and step into your power with confidence and courage. Repeat this incantation regularly to reinforce your connection to your inner power and to continue awakening and expanding it.

Incantation for Clearing Energy Blockages

In the realm of energy, I now reside,
To clear the blockages that reside inside.
With focused intent and magic's embrace,
I release what hinders, creating sacred space.

I call upon the forces that flow so free,
To cleanse and purify, let energy be.
From the Earth below and the heavens above,
I summon their power, divine love.

I invoke the fire, the element of transformation,
To burn away blockages, with fierce determination.
With flames ablaze, I release all that's stuck,
Clearing the path, like wildfire's luck.

I call upon the waters, flowing and pure,
To wash away obstacles, a cleansing allure.
From rivers and streams, let the currents sweep,
Dissolving blockages, a journey so deep.

I summon the winds, with their gusts and gales,
To carry away stagnation, like ships with sails.
With each breath, they blow and cleanse,
Removing blockages, creating space immense.

I invoke the Earth, stable and strong,
To ground and support, as energy moves along.
From deep within, let roots grow deep,
Clearing the blockages, a fertile leap.

I connect with the ethers, the realm of the unseen,
To dissolve energetic barriers, so serene.
With cosmic light, I shine and infuse,
Clearing blockages, as energy renews.

By the power of intention and ancient lore,
I clear energy blockages, forevermore.
With each word spoken and every thought held,
I release what hinders, energies compelled.

As the incantation echoes through time and space,
I release all blockages, with divine grace.
I am open and free, my energy flows,
Clearing blockages, as transformation grows.

So mote it be, as I declare this decree,
I clear energy blockages, so mote it be.
I am aligned and in harmony,
Free from blockages, I am truly free.

Note: As you recite this incantation, visualize the energy blockages within you dissolving and being carried away. Feel the elements and their respective qualities supporting and assisting in the clearing process. Set the intention to release any stagnant or negative energies that may be blocking your flow. Allow the energy to flow freely and smoothly throughout your being as you affirm your alignment and harmony. Repeat this incantation as needed to clear energy blockages and maintain a balanced and harmonious energetic state.

Incantation for Opening the Third Eye

In the realm of sight unseen,
I call upon forces ancient and keen.
Open the gate to the sacred sight,
Awaken the Third Eye, shining bright.

With this incantation, I do decree,
Unlock the vision that lies within me.
Pineal gland, awaken and perceive,
The hidden truths I'm ready to receive.

The Third Eye's vision, clear and true,
I welcome the insights it will imbue.
Seeing beyond the physical realm,
Intuition guides, taking the helm.

Mysteries unravel, veils are lifted,
Perception expanded, awareness gifted.
The inner eye, a beacon of light,
Guiding me through the day and night.

As I chant these words, let it be so,
The Third Eye opens, its power will grow.
Illuminate the path of knowledge and sight,
Grant me wisdom, with clarity and might.

By the ancient forces, I'm guided and led,
Awakening the Third Eye, where knowledge is spread.
I embrace the visions, the wisdom they bestow,
The Third Eye opens, and I am ready to know.

Note: When performing the incantation for opening the Third Eye, create a calm and sacred space for yourself. Close your eyes and focus your attention on the area between your eyebrows, where the Third Eye is said to reside. Take deep breaths and relax your body and mind. Visualize a vibrant, indigo-colored light radiating from your Third Eye, growing brighter and more intense with each breath. As you chant the incantation, feel the energy of the words resonate within you, activating and awakening your Third Eye. Embrace the sensations and insights that may arise during or after the incantation. Trust in the process and allow your intuition to guide you on your journey of expanded consciousness.

Incantation for Enhancing Psychic Protection

By the ancient forces that guard and guide,
I call upon protection, strong and wide.
With psychic senses keen and sharp,
I shield myself from all that may harm.

Invisible walls, a fortress around me,
Repelling negativity, setting me free.
No ill intent shall find its way,
As I walk this path, day by day.

With the power of my spirit and mind,
I block unwanted energies, I leave them behind.
No psychic attacks shall penetrate,
My protection stands firm, early and late.

I call upon the guardians of the unseen,
To bolster my defenses, keen and keen.
Wrap me in a cloak of divine light,
Shielding my aura, keeping me bright.

Negative thoughts, I banish away,
In their place, positive energy will stay.
No harmful influences shall take hold,
My psychic protection remains bold.

With this incantation, I empower my soul,
Creating a shield that makes me whole.
No harm shall reach me, body or mind,
Psychic protection, forever bind.

Note: When performing the incantation for enhancing psychic protection, find a quiet and sacred space where you can focus your energy and intention. Visualize yourself surrounded by a luminous shield of light, impenetrable to negative energies or psychic attacks. Speak the incantation with confidence and clarity, infusing it with your intent to strengthen your psychic defenses. Feel the energy of the words resonate within you, reinforcing your psychic protection. Regularly reaffirm your intention and strengthen your psychic protection to maintain your energetic boundaries. Trust in the power of your own psychic abilities and the support of the unseen forces as you enhance your psychic protection.

Chapter 3
Spells

Exploring Ancient Babylon's Rituals

Spell of Elemental Conjuring

Tools:

Four colored candles representing the elements:
Red for Fire
Blue for Water
Green for Earth
Yellow for Air
An incense burner and corresponding incense for each element:
Frankincense for Fire
Sandalwood for Water
Patchouli for Earth
Lavender for Air
A small dish or cloth representing the altar or sacred space
Crystals or gemstones associated with each element:
Carnelian or Ruby for Fire
Aquamarine or Amethyst for Water
Moss Agate or Green Aventurine for Earth
Clear Quartz or Selenite for Air
A small cauldron or fire-safe bowl
A lighter or matches
A journal or paper and pen
Instructions:

Preparation:

Find a quiet and peaceful space where you can perform the spell undisturbed.
Set up your altar or sacred space by placing the dish or cloth in the center.
Arrange the colored candles around the dish, with the corresponding crystals placed beside each candle.
Place the incense burner at the center of the altar.

Cleansing and Grounding:

Light the incense corresponding to the element of Fire (Frankincense) and let the smoke purify the space.
Take a moment to ground yourself by taking deep breaths and focusing on your connection to the Earth.
Elemental Invocation:

Stand before the altar and light the red candle representing Fire.

Hold the carnelian or ruby crystal in your hand and say the following invocation:

> "Oh, Divine Fire, element of passion and transformation,
> I invoke your essence and sacred flame.
> Fill this space with your radiant energy,
> And let your fiery presence be felt."

Connecting with Fire:

Sit or stand before the lit candle and crystal, feeling the warmth and energy of the Fire element.
Visualize flames dancing before you, flickering and illuminating the darkness.
Focus on your intention to connect with the element of Fire and its qualities of passion, transformation, and creativity.

Elemental Offerings:

Take a small piece of paper and write down any fears, doubts, or limitations you wish to transform.
Hold the paper in your hands and infuse it with your intention to release these negative energies.
Place the paper in the cauldron or fire-safe bowl and carefully light it with the flame of the candle.
As the paper burns, visualize your fears and limitations being transformed by the purifying power of Fire.
Take a moment to express gratitude for the release and transformation.

Elemental Invocation (Continued):

Extinguish the red candle and light the blue candle representing Water.

Hold the aquamarine or amethyst crystal in your hand and say the following invocation:

> "Oh, Sacred Water, element of emotions and intuition,
> I invoke your essence and flowing currents.
> Let your soothing and purifying waters cleanse my being,
> And guide me on a path of emotional balance and intuition."

Connecting with Water:

Sit or stand before the lit candle and crystal, visualizing a calm and serene body of water.
Feel the coolness and fluidity of the Water element, allowing it to wash away any emotional tension or imbalance.
Focus on your intention to connect with the element of Water and its qualities of emotional healing, intuition, and adaptability.

Elemental Offerings:

Take a moment to reflect on any emotional wounds or challenges you wish to heal and release.
Visualize these emotions being carried away by the gentle flow of a river or the crashing waves of the ocean.
Take the piece of paper with your intentions and submerge it in a bowl of water, symbolizing the release and purification of emotions.
Express gratitude for the healing and emotional balance you seek.

Elemental Invocation (Continued):

Extinguish the blue candle and light the green candle representing Earth.

Hold the moss agate or green aventurine crystal in your hand and say the following invocation:

"Oh, Sacred Earth, element of stability and grounding,
I invoke your essence and nurturing embrace.
Let your abundant energy support and nourish my being,
And guide me on a path of growth and stability."

Connecting with Earth:

Sit or stand before the lit candle and crystal, imagining yourself rooted deeply in the Earth.
Feel the stability and grounding energy of the Earth element, anchoring you to the present moment.
Focus on your intention to connect with the element of Earth and its qualities of stability, growth, and abundance.

Elemental Offerings:

Reflect on any areas of your life where you seek stability and growth.

Take a handful of earth or soil and hold it in your hands, infusing it with your intentions for abundance and stability.
Sprinkle the earth or soil onto the altar, symbolizing your connection to the nurturing energy of the Earth.
Express gratitude for the stability and growth that you wish to manifest.

Elemental Invocation (Continued):

Extinguish the green candle and light the yellow candle representing Air.

Hold the clear quartz or selenite crystal in your hand and say the following invocation:

> "Oh, Divine Air, element of communication and clarity,
> I invoke your essence and gentle breeze.
> Let your refreshing currents sweep away mental fog,
> And guide me on a path of clear thoughts and inspired ideas."

Connecting with Air:

Sit or stand before the lit candle and crystal, envisioning a gentle breeze blowing through the air.
Feel the lightness and clarity of the Air element, allowing it to clear away mental clutter and bring fresh inspiration.
Focus on your intention to connect with the element of Air and its qualities of clear thinking, communication, and inspiration.

Elemental Offerings:

Take a moment to reflect on any mental blocks or confusion you wish to release.
Write down any limiting beliefs or negative thought patterns that you want to let go of.
Hold the paper with your intentions and allow the wind or a gentle breeze to pass over it, symbolizing the dispersal of mental fog.
Burn the paper in the cauldron or fire-safe bowl, visualizing the release of negative thoughts and the space being cleared for clarity and inspiration.
Express gratitude for the clarity of mind and inspired ideas you seek.

Closing the Ritual:

Extinguish the yellow candle, completing the elemental invocation.
Take a moment to offer gratitude to the elements and their energies for their presence and assistance.
Reflect on the experience and the intentions you have set during the ritual.

Record any insights or experiences in your journal or on paper, allowing yourself to integrate the energies and guidance received.

Remember, this spell is intended for personal use and empowerment. Approach it with respect, mindfulness, and a clear intention. Adapt the tools and materials as needed to align with your personal practice and beliefs.

Spell for Transmutation of Energy

Tools:

A white candle representing purity and divine energy
A black candle representing transformation and transmutation
A small cauldron or fire-safe bowl
A lighter or matches
A small piece of paper and a pen
Optional: crystals or gemstones associated with transmutation, such as labradorite, obsidian, or amethyst
Instructions:

Preparation:

Find a quiet and sacred space where you can perform the spell without distractions.
Set up your altar or sacred space by placing the white candle on the left and the black candle on the right.
Place the cauldron or fire-safe bowl between the candles.
If using crystals, arrange them around the cauldron or place them near the candles.

Cleansing and Grounding:

Take a moment to center yourself and connect with your breath.
Ground yourself by envisioning roots growing from the soles of your feet into the earth, anchoring you to its stable energy.
Light the white candle, representing purity and divine energy.
Allow the light of the candle to cleanse and purify your space and energy.

Setting Intentions:

Take the small piece of paper and write down the energy or situation you wish to transmute.
Be specific and concise in your words, focusing on the aspect of energy that you want to transform.
For example, you could write "I transmute fear into courage" or "I transmute negativity into positivity."
Visualize this energy or situation being transformed into its positive counterpart.

Invocation and Affirmation:

Light the black candle, representing transformation and transmutation.

Hold the paper with your written intention in front of the black candle and say the following invocation:

> "By the power of transformation and the alchemy of fire,
> I invoke the energy of transmutation to manifest my desire.
> With this flame, I transmute (state your intention),
> Turning darkness into light and empowering my spirit's flight."

Repeat the affirmation three times, allowing the words to resonate deeply within you.

Visualize the black candle's flame growing brighter and more intense, symbolizing the transformative power of transmutation.

Burning and Release:

Carefully place the paper with your intention into the cauldron or fire-safe bowl.
Hold the paper with a pair of tongs or use a fire-safe tool to ignite it with the flame of the black candle.
As the paper burns, visualize the energy or situation being consumed by the flames, turning into ashes.
Feel a sense of release and liberation as the negative energy is transmuted into positive, transformative energy.

Gratitude and Grounding:

Once the paper has completely burned, take a moment to express gratitude for the transmutation and release of energy.
Thank the universe, your guides, or any spiritual entities you resonate with for their assistance in this process.
Close your eyes and take a few deep breaths, allowing yourself to feel grounded and present in the moment.

Closing the Ritual:

Extinguish both the white and black candles, symbolizing the completion of the transmutation process.
You may choose to leave the crystals on your altar as a reminder of the transmutative energy you have invoked.

Reflect on the experience and the energy shift that you have initiated.
Trust that the transmutation process has been set in motion and remain open to the positive changes that will unfold.

Remember, this spell is intended for personal use and empowerment. Approach it with respect, mindfulness, and a clear intention. Adapt the tools and materials as needed to align with your personal practice and beliefs.

Spell for Astral Projection and Soul Travel

Tools:

A purple candle representing spiritual awareness and connection
A small piece of amethyst or clear quartz crystal
A small cauldron or fire-safe bowl
A lighter or matches
A comfortable and quiet space for meditation
Optional: essential oils or incense associated with spiritual exploration, such as lavender or frankincense

Instructions:

Preparation:

Find a quiet and sacred space where you can perform the spell without distractions.
Set up your altar or sacred space by placing the purple candle in the center and the crystal near it.
Place the cauldron or fire-safe bowl in front of the candle.

Cleansing and Grounding:

Take a moment to center yourself and connect with your breath.
Ground yourself by envisioning roots growing from the soles of your feet into the earth, anchoring you to its stable energy.
Light the purple candle, representing spiritual awareness and connection.
Allow the light of the candle to cleanse and purify your space and energy.

Setting Intentions:

Hold the crystal in your hand and close your eyes.
State your intention clearly and concisely, such as "I am ready to explore the realms beyond the physical and experience astral projection."
Visualize yourself surrounded by a protective, purple aura, shielding and supporting your astral journey.

Invocation and Affirmation:

Gaze into the flame of the purple candle and say the following invocation:

"With this flame of sacred light,
I call upon the powers of day and night.
Grant me the ability to travel afar,
To soar beyond the realms, like a shining star."

Repeat the affirmation three times, allowing the words to resonate deeply within you.

Visualize yourself leaving your physical body and ascending into the astral realm with ease and grace.

Meditation and Visualization:

Sit comfortably in a meditative posture and close your eyes.
Take a few deep breaths, relaxing your body and clearing your mind.
Visualize yourself floating above your physical body, detached and weightless.
Feel the sensation of freedom and expansion as you explore the astral plane.
Focus on any specific destination or experience you wish to encounter during your astral journey.

Protection and Guidance:

Envision a shield of divine light surrounding you, providing protection and guidance throughout your astral projection.
Call upon any spiritual guides, ancestors, or higher beings you resonate with to accompany and assist you on your journey.
Trust in their presence and guidance as you navigate the astral realms.

Return and Grounding:

When you feel ready to return, visualize yourself gently descending back into your physical body.
Take a few moments to integrate your experiences and ground yourself in the present moment.
Express gratitude to your guides and the universe for the opportunity to explore the astral realms.

Closing the Ritual:

Extinguish the purple candle, symbolizing the completion of the astral projection spell.
Place the crystal in the cauldron or fire-safe bowl as an offering of thanks and grounding energy.

Reflect on your experience and journal any insights or messages you received during your astral journey.

Remember, astral projection and soul travel require practice, patience, and a deep understanding of your own spiritual abilities. Approach this spell with respect, mindfulness, and a clear intention. Adapt the tools and materials as needed to align with your personal practice and beliefs.

Spell for Banishing Negative Influences

Tools:

A black candle representing protection and banishment
A small piece of obsidian or black tourmaline crystal
A small cauldron or fire-safe bowl
A lighter or matches
A piece of paper and a pen
Optional: protective herbs such as sage or rosemary, and essential oils or incense associated with purification, such as frankincense or cedarwood

Instructions:

Preparation:

Find a quiet and undisturbed space where you can perform the spell.
Set up your altar or sacred space by placing the black candle in the center and the crystal near it.
Place the cauldron or fire-safe bowl in front of the candle.

Cleansing and Grounding:

Take a moment to ground yourself by connecting with your breath and focusing on your intention to banish negative influences.
Light the black candle, representing protection and banishment.
If you have chosen to use herbs or incense, light them as well, allowing the smoke to purify the space.

Writing your Intentions:

Take the piece of paper and the pen and write down the negative influences or energies you wish to banish from your life.
Be specific and clear in your descriptions, expressing your desire to release and be free from these influences.

Invocation and Affirmation:

Hold the crystal in your hand and close your eyes.
State your intention clearly and powerfully, such as "I banish all negative influences from my life. I am free and protected."

Visualize a sphere of protective energy forming around you, shielding you from the negative influences you wish to banish.

Burning the Negative Influences:

Light the piece of paper with the flame of the black candle.
As the paper burns, visualize the negative influences being consumed by the fire and transformed into positive energy.
Place the burning paper into the cauldron or fire-safe bowl, allowing it to burn completely.

Affirmation and Release:

While the paper burns, recite the following affirmation three times:

"By the power of fire and the strength within,
I banish the negative and let new beginnings begin.
No longer shall these influences hold sway,
I release them now, forever and a day."

Feel the weight of the negative influences being lifted from your spirit as you recite the affirmation.

Cleansing and Protection:

Hold the crystal in your hand and envision its protective energy surrounding you, forming a shield against any future negative influences.
Express gratitude to the crystal and the elements for their assistance in the banishing process.

Closing the Ritual:

Extinguish the black candle, symbolizing the completion of the banishing spell.
If you have used herbs or incense, allow them to burn out completely or safely extinguish them.
Take a few moments to ground yourself and center your energy.
Dispose of the ashes from the burned paper, either by burying them in the earth or scattering them to the wind.

Remember, the power of the spell comes from within you and your intention. Approach this spell with focus, clarity, and determination. Adapt the tools and materials as needed to align with your personal practice and beliefs.

Spell for Divination with Sacred Cards

Tools:

A deck of tarot cards or oracle cards (choose one that resonates with you)
A quiet and peaceful space
A cloth or altar to lay out the cards
Optional: a candle, incense, or other items to create a sacred atmosphere
Instructions:

Preparation:

Find a quiet and comfortable space where you can perform the spell without distractions. If desired, set up your altar or sacred space by placing the cloth and any additional items that enhance your connection to the divine.

Grounding and Intention:

Take a few deep breaths to center yourself and clear your mind.
Hold the deck of cards in your hands and close your eyes.
State your intention clearly and powerfully, such as "I seek divine guidance and insight through this card reading."

Shuffling the Cards:

Shuffle the deck while focusing on your question or the area of your life you wish to explore.
Allow your intuition to guide your shuffling, trusting that the right cards will be drawn for your divination.

Drawing the Cards:

When you feel ready, cut the deck into three separate piles.
Reassemble the deck, combining the piles in any order that feels intuitive to you.
Begin drawing the cards one by one, laying them face up on the cloth or altar in a spread of your choice.

Interpreting the Cards:

Take a moment to observe the cards and their positions in the spread.
Pay attention to your intuition, the symbols, and the meanings associated with each card.

Use your knowledge of the cards and any guidebook or reference material you have to interpret their messages.
Trust your inner guidance and the messages that come through as you connect with the cards.

Divine Insight:

Reflect on the messages and insights provided by the cards.
Ask yourself questions related to the reading and contemplate the guidance you have received.
Take notes if desired to capture important insights or impressions.

Closing the Reading:

Express gratitude to the divine, the cards, and any spiritual guides or beings you work with.
If desired, you can conclude with a closing affirmation or prayer, thanking the cards for their guidance and requesting continued support and clarity in your journey.

Remember, the cards are a tool to tap into your own intuition and the wisdom of the divine. Approach your card reading with an open mind and heart, and trust the messages that come through. Practice regularly to develop your skills and deepen your connection to the cards and the insights they provide.

Spell for Healing Physical Ailments

Tools:

A white or green candle
Healing crystals (such as amethyst, clear quartz, or rose quartz)
Healing herbs (such as lavender, chamomile, or eucalyptus)
A small bowl of salt or saltwater
Optional: a healing oil or essential oil blend

Instructions:

Preparation:

Find a quiet and comfortable space where you can perform the spell without interruptions.
Set up your altar or sacred space by placing the candle, crystals, herbs, and bowl of salt within reach.

Grounding and Centering:

Close your eyes and take a few deep breaths to ground yourself and clear your mind.
Visualize a healing white light surrounding you, providing protection and support during the spell.

Candle Dedication:

Take the white or green candle and hold it in your hands.
State your intention clearly and powerfully, such as "I dedicate this candle to heal and restore my physical body."

Candle Blessing:

Light the candle and focus your attention on the flame.
Envision the flame as a source of healing energy, radiating warmth and light.
Say the following incantation or create your own:

> "By the power of ancient ways,
> I call upon healing rays.
> Body, mend and be made whole,
> Restore my health, my being, my soul."

Crystal and Herb Infusion:

Hold the healing crystals in your hands and visualize them filling with healing energy.
Place the crystals around the lit candle, forming a circle or arrangement.
Sprinkle the healing herbs around the crystals and candle, infusing the space with their scent and properties.

Salt Cleansing:

Dip your fingers into the bowl of salt or saltwater.
Gently touch your forehead, throat, and heart, envisioning the salt purifying and cleansing your body.

Healing Affirmation:

Repeat the following affirmation or create your own, speaking it with conviction:

> "With every breath, I heal and restore,
> Vibrant health flows through every pore.
> My body is a temple, strong and whole,
> Healing energy nurtures every cell, every soul."

Healing Visualization:

Close your eyes and visualize a vibrant and radiant light surrounding the area of your body that needs healing.
Imagine this light penetrating deeply, dissolving any blockages or ailments, and promoting healing and vitality.

Closing:

Express gratitude to the divine, the elements, and any spiritual guides or beings you work with.
Allow the candle to burn safely or extinguish it, knowing that the healing energy has been set in motion.

Remember, this spell is meant to complement and support any medical treatments or therapies you may be receiving. It is essential to consult with healthcare professionals for serious or persistent physical ailments. Trust in the power of healing and your body's innate ability to restore itself to a state of well-being.

Spell for Love and Attraction

Tools:

A pink or red candle
Love-enhancing crystals (such as rose quartz, rhodochrosite, or garnet)
Love herbs (such as rose petals, lavender, or cinnamon)
A small piece of paper or parchment
Red or pink ink pen
Optional: love oil or essential oil blend

Instructions:

Preparation:

Find a quiet and undisturbed space where you can perform the spell.
Set up your altar or sacred space by placing the candle, crystals, herbs, and paper within reach.

Setting Intentions:

Close your eyes and take a few deep breaths to center yourself.
Reflect on your intention for the spell, whether it's attracting new love, enhancing an existing relationship, or finding soulmate connection.

Candle Dedication:

Take the pink or red candle and hold it in your hands.
State your intention clearly and powerfully, such as "I dedicate this candle to manifest love and attraction in my life."

Candle Blessing:

Light the candle and focus your attention on the flame.
Envision the flame as a beacon of love and attraction, drawing in the energy and essence of your desires.
Say the following incantation or create your own:

> "By the light of this sacred fire,
> Love and attraction I now inspire.
> Open my heart, ignite the spark,

Draw to me love, both deep and true, to embark."

Crystal and Herb Arrangement:

Hold the love-enhancing crystals in your hands and infuse them with your intention.
Place the crystals around the lit candle, creating a circle or arrangement.
Sprinkle the love herbs around the crystals and candle, invoking their fragrance and properties.

Love Invocation:

Take the piece of paper or parchment and write down your desired qualities or traits you seek in a partner.
Use the red or pink ink pen to write with intention and focus on your heartfelt desires.

Affirmation and Visualization:

Hold the paper in your hands and close your eyes.
Repeat the following affirmation or create your own, infusing it with sincere emotion:
"Love flows to me, effortlessly and true,
I attract the love that I desire, through and through.
Hearts align, souls entwine,
Love and attraction, forever mine."

Visualize yourself radiating with love and attracting the ideal partner or deepening the bond in an existing relationship.
See yourself surrounded by love and feel the joy and fulfillment that comes with it.

Charging the Paper:

Hold the paper over the candle flame, allowing it to catch fire briefly.
Safely extinguish the flame, ensuring the paper is not completely burned.
Visualize the energy of your intention infusing the paper.

Closing:

Express gratitude to the divine, the elements, and any spiritual guides or beings you work with.
Allow the candle to burn safely or extinguish it, knowing that the energy of love and attraction has been set in motion.
Remember, this spell is intended to enhance and support your efforts in attracting love and deepening connections. It's essential to be open and receptive to love opportunities

that align with your highest good. Focus on cultivating self-love and being the best version of yourself to attract positive relationships into your life.

Spell for Protection Against Dark Forces

Tools:

A black candle
Protective crystals (such as black tourmaline, obsidian, or amethyst)
Protective herbs (such as sage, frankincense, or rosemary)
A small piece of paper or parchment
Black ink pen
Salt or protective oil (optional)

Instructions:

Preparation:

Find a quiet and undisturbed space where you can perform the spell.
Set up your altar or sacred space by placing the candle, crystals, herbs, and paper within reach.

Setting Intentions:

Close your eyes and take a few deep breaths to center yourself.
Reflect on your intention for the spell, which is to protect yourself against dark forces, negative energies, or harmful influences.

Candle Dedication:

Take the black candle and hold it in your hands.
State your intention clearly and powerfully, such as "I dedicate this candle to ward off and protect against dark forces and negative energies."

Candle Blessing:

Light the black candle and focus your attention on the flame.
Visualize the flame as a source of powerful protection, creating a shield around you.
Say the following incantation or create your own:

> "Candle of black, strong and true,
> Ward off darkness, protect what's true.
> Shield me from harm, keep me safe,
> Banish the shadows, bring divine grace."

Crystal and Herb Arrangement:

Hold the protective crystals in your hands and infuse them with your intention.
Place the crystals around the lit candle, creating a circle or arrangement.
Sprinkle the protective herbs around the crystals and candle, invoking their purifying and shielding properties.

Protection Invocation:

Take the piece of paper or parchment and write down your intention for protection against dark forces or negative energies.
Use the black ink pen to write with determination and focus.

Affirmation and Visualization:

Hold the paper in your hands and close your eyes.
Repeat the following affirmation or create your own, infusing it with a sense of inner power and protection:

> "I am shielded, I am strong,
> Protected from all that is wrong.
> Dark forces flee, negative energies cease,
> I am safe, in divine peace."

Visualize yourself surrounded by a powerful shield of light, repelling any dark forces or negative influences.
Feel the strength and security of this protective energy enveloping you completely.

Charging the Paper:

Hold the paper over the candle flame, allowing it to catch fire briefly.
Safely extinguish the flame, ensuring the paper is not completely burned.
Visualize the energy of your intention infusing the paper.

Closing:

Express gratitude to the divine, the elements, and any spiritual guides or beings you work with.
Place the paper in a safe and sacred space or bury it in the earth, symbolizing the anchoring of your protection.
Allow the candle to burn safely or extinguish it, knowing that you are protected and shielded from dark forces.

Remember, this spell is intended to strengthen your personal energetic boundaries and protect you from negative influences. It's important to cultivate positive energy, practice self-care, and be mindful of the environments and people you engage with. Trust in the power of your intention and the divine protection surrounding you.

Spell for Enhancing Intuition and Psychic Abilities

Tools:

Purple candle
Amethyst crystal
Lavender or mugwort herb
A small piece of paper or parchment
Purple ink pen
Divination tool (tarot cards, runes, pendulum, etc.)

Instructions:

Preparation:

Find a quiet and comfortable space where you can focus and perform the spell undisturbed.
Set up your altar or sacred space by placing the candle, amethyst crystal, herb, and divination tool within reach.

Setting Intentions:

Close your eyes, take a few deep breaths, and allow yourself to relax and enter a meditative state.
Reflect on your intention for the spell, which is to enhance your intuition and psychic abilities, to gain deeper insights and guidance.

Candle Dedication:

Take the purple candle in your hands and hold it up to your heart.
State your intention clearly and passionately, such as "I dedicate this candle to enhance my intuition and open the channels of psychic perception."

Candle Blessing:

Light the purple candle and focus your attention on the flame.
Visualize the flame as a source of divine wisdom, illuminating your path and opening your inner sight.
Say the following incantation or create your own:

> "Candle of purple, light the way,
> Enhance my intuition, guide my way.
> Open the doors to psychic sight,
> Reveal the truths hidden from sight."

Crystal and Herb Activation:

Hold the amethyst crystal in your hands and infuse it with your intention.
Place the crystal near the lit candle, allowing its energy to interact with the flame and surrounding aura.
Sprinkle a small amount of lavender or mugwort herb around the crystal and candle, invoking their properties of heightened awareness and spiritual connection.

Divination Tool Alignment:

Hold your chosen divination tool in your hands and connect with its energy.
State your intention for the tool, asking it to assist you in accessing your intuition and receiving clear guidance.
Place the divination tool near the candle and crystal, aligning it with their energies.

Affirmation and Visualization:

Take the piece of paper or parchment and write down your affirmation for enhancing intuition and psychic abilities.
Use the purple ink pen to write with intention and focus.
Read the affirmation aloud, infusing it with belief and determination.

Activation Ritual:

Hold the paper in your hands and close your eyes.
Repeat the following incantation or create your own, channeling the energy of your intention:

> "With divine guidance, my intuition awakes,
> Psychic abilities strengthen, my spirit takes.
> Open the doors, expand my mind,
> Insights and wisdom, now intertwined."

Visualize your intuition growing stronger, like a vibrant purple light expanding within you.
Feel the connection with higher realms and the wisdom of the universe flowing through you.

Charging the Paper:

Hold the paper over the candle flame, allowing it to catch fire briefly.
Safely extinguish the flame, ensuring the paper is not completely burned.
Visualize the energy of your intention infusing the paper.

Divination and Intuition Practice:

Use your chosen divination tool to perform a reading or seek guidance.
Trust your intuition and allow the insights to flow naturally.
Take note of any symbols, feelings, or messages that come to you during the practice.
Closing:
Express gratitude to the divine, the elements, and any spiritual guides or beings you work with.
Safely extinguish the candle, knowing that your intuition and psychic abilities have been enhanced.
Keep the charged paper and amethyst crystal in a safe and sacred space, using them as reminders of your intention and tools for ongoing connection with your intuition.

Remember, developing intuition and psychic abilities takes time, practice, and trust. This spell is a catalyst to help you align with your innate gifts, but it's important to continue cultivating your intuition through meditation, journaling, and regular divination practices. Stay open to the messages you receive and honor your intuitive insights.

Spell for Amplifying Magical Power

Tools:

Red candle
Clear quartz crystal
Cinnamon or ginger herb
A small piece of paper or parchment
Red ink pen
A small cauldron or fire-safe container

Instructions:

Preparation:

Find a quiet and undisturbed space where you can focus and perform the spell.
Set up your altar or sacred space by placing the red candle, clear quartz crystal, herb, and cauldron within reach.

Setting Intentions:

Close your eyes, take a few deep breaths, and center yourself.
Reflect on your intention for the spell, which is to amplify your magical power and enhance the effectiveness of your spells and rituals.

Candle Dedication:

Take the red candle in your hands and hold it up to your heart.
State your intention clearly and passionately, such as "I dedicate this candle to amplify my magical power and manifest my desires with great strength."

Candle Blessing:

Light the red candle and focus your attention on the flame.
Visualize the flame as a source of potent and vibrant energy, radiating power and strength.
Say the following incantation or create your own:

> "Flame of red, burning bright,
> Amplify my power with your fiery light.
> Energize my spells, make them strong,

As I will it, so mote it be, ere long."

Crystal and Herb Activation:

Hold the clear quartz crystal in your hands and infuse it with your intention.
Place the crystal near the lit candle, allowing its energy to interact with the flame and surrounding aura.
Sprinkle a small amount of cinnamon or ginger herb around the crystal and candle, invoking their properties of energy amplification and empowerment.

Affirmation and Visualization:

Take the piece of paper or parchment and write down your affirmation for amplifying your magical power.
Use the red ink pen to write with intention and focus.
Read the affirmation aloud, infusing it with belief and determination.

Activation Ritual:

Hold the paper in your hands and close your eyes.
Repeat the following incantation or create your own, channeling the energy of your intention:

> "Magical power, rise and surge,
> Amplify my will, let it emerge.
> By the flame's heat and crystal's might,
> I command my magic to take flight."

Visualize your magical power growing and expanding, like waves of vibrant energy radiating from your core.

Charging the Paper:

Hold the paper over the candle flame, allowing it to catch fire.
Safely drop the burning paper into the cauldron or fire-safe container.
Visualize the energy of your intention being released and intensified as the paper burns.

Crystal Connection:

Take the clear quartz crystal and pass it through the smoke of the extinguished paper, cleansing and charging it with the amplified energy.
Empowered Spells and Rituals:

Whenever you perform spells or rituals, hold the clear quartz crystal in your hand or place it on your altar to enhance the power and effectiveness of your magic.

Closing:
Express gratitude to the divine, the elements, and any spiritual guides or beings you work with.
Safely extinguish the candle, knowing that your magical power has been amplified and your spells will be potent.

Remember, the true source of your magical power resides within you. This spell serves as a catalyst to awaken and amplify that power. Use it responsibly, always aligned with your highest good and the good of others. Regularly practice connecting with your inner magic through meditation, visualization, and other spiritual practices.

Spell for Enhancing Beauty and Youthfulness

Tools:

Pink or rose-colored candle
Rose quartz crystal
Lavender or rose petals
A small hand mirror
A small jar or container
Coconut oil or rose oil

Instructions:

Preparation:

Find a quiet and comfortable space where you can perform the spell without interruption.
Set up your altar or sacred space by placing the pink candle, rose quartz crystal, petals, hand mirror, and jar within reach.

Setting Intentions:

Close your eyes, take a few deep breaths, and center yourself.
Reflect on your intention for the spell, which is to enhance your beauty and promote a youthful appearance.

Candle Dedication:

Hold the pink candle in your hands and visualize it as a symbol of beauty and youthfulness.
State your intention clearly and passionately, such as "I dedicate this candle to enhance my beauty and radiate youthful energy."

Candle Blessing:

Light the pink candle and focus your attention on the flame.
Visualize the flame as a gentle and warm light that infuses your body with beauty and youthfulness.
Say the following incantation or create your own:

"Candle of pink, radiant and bright,

Enhance my beauty, restore my light.
Youthful energy, come my way,
As I will it, so mote it be, I say."

Crystal and Petal Activation:

Hold the rose quartz crystal in your hands and infuse it with your intention.
Place the crystal near the lit candle, allowing its loving energy to blend with the flame.
Scatter the lavender or rose petals around the candle and crystal, symbolizing beauty and grace.

Mirror Affirmation:

Hold the hand mirror and gaze into your own eyes, connecting with your inner beauty and essence.
Repeat affirmations that enhance your perception of beauty and youthfulness.
Speak from your heart, expressing love and gratitude for your unique qualities.

Anointing Ritual:

Take the small jar or container and fill it with coconut oil or rose oil.
Hold the jar in your hands and visualize it being infused with the energy of beauty and youth.
Dip your fingertips into the oil and gently anoint your face, focusing on areas you wish to enhance or rejuvenate.
As you apply the oil, envision the oil nourishing your skin, bringing forth a youthful glow and radiance.

Gratitude and Release:

Express gratitude to the divine, the elements, and any spiritual guides or beings you work with.
Blow out the candle, releasing the energy of your intention into the universe.
Place the rose quartz crystal and petals in a special place, such as your altar or a sacred space, to serve as a reminder of your beauty and youthfulness.

Remember, true beauty comes from within, and this spell is intended to enhance and highlight the natural beauty and radiance you already possess. Use this spell as a way to connect with your inner beauty, embrace self-love, and radiate confidence. Emphasize self-care practices, nourishing your body and mind with healthy habits, and embracing your unique qualities.

Spell for Manifesting Wealth and Abundance

Tools:

Green candle
Citrine crystal
Cinnamon or basil herbs
A small dish or bowl
A small piece of paper
Pen or pencil

Instructions:

Preparation:

Find a quiet and comfortable space where you can perform the spell without interruption.
Set up your altar or sacred space by placing the green candle, citrine crystal, herbs, dish or bowl, and a small piece of paper within reach.

Setting Intentions:

Close your eyes, take a few deep breaths, and center yourself.
Reflect on your intention for the spell, which is to manifest wealth and abundance in your life.

Candle Dedication:

Hold the green candle in your hands and visualize it as a symbol of financial prosperity and abundance.
State your intention clearly and passionately, such as "I dedicate this candle to manifest wealth and abundance in my life."

Candle Blessing:

Light the green candle and focus your attention on the flame.
Visualize the flame as a vibrant and powerful source of financial abundance.
Say the following incantation or create your own:

> "Candle of green, shining bright,
> Manifest abundance, day and night.

Wealth and riches, come my way,
As I will it, so mote it be, I say."

Crystal and Herb Activation:

Hold the citrine crystal in your hands and infuse it with your intention.
Place the crystal near the lit candle, allowing its vibrant energy to blend with the flame.
Sprinkle a small amount of cinnamon or basil herbs into the dish or bowl, symbolizing abundance and prosperity.

Writing Affirmations:

Take the small piece of paper and write down your financial goals and desires.
Be specific and positive in your affirmations, focusing on what you want to attract into your life.
For example, you could write, "I attract abundant opportunities for wealth and financial success."

Paper Charging:

Hold the piece of paper in your hands and visualize your goals and desires coming to fruition.
Visualize yourself already in possession of the wealth and abundance you seek.
Hold the paper near the candle flame, allowing it to receive the energy of the flame and the intention you have set.

Gratitude and Release:

Express gratitude to the divine, the elements, and any spiritual guides or beings you work with.
Burn the small piece of paper in the candle flame, releasing your intentions to the universe.
As the paper burns, visualize your goals and desires manifesting in your life, feeling a sense of gratitude and excitement.

Closing:

Thank the elements and any spiritual guides or beings you invoked during the spell.
Blow out the candle, symbolizing the completion of the spell.
Keep the citrine crystal in a prominent place or carry it with you as a reminder of your intention to manifest wealth and abundance.

Remember, this spell is a tool to help align your energy and intentions with the manifestation of wealth and abundance. It is essential to take practical steps in your daily life to support your financial goals, such as budgeting, saving, investing wisely, and seeking opportunities for growth. Embrace a mindset of abundance, gratitude, and generosity as you work towards manifesting wealth in your life.

Spell for Breaking Hexes and Curses

Tools:

Black candle
Amethyst or obsidian crystal
Salt
A small dish or bowl
A small piece of paper
Pen or pencil
Instructions:

Preparation:

Find a quiet and undisturbed space where you can perform the spell.
Set up your altar or sacred space by placing the black candle, amethyst or obsidian crystal, salt, dish or bowl, and a small piece of paper within reach.

Setting Intentions:

Close your eyes, take a few deep breaths, and center yourself.
Reflect on your intention for the spell, which is to break any hexes or curses that may be affecting you.

Candle Dedication:

Hold the black candle in your hands and visualize it as a powerful tool for breaking negative energies and curses.
State your intention clearly and strongly, such as "I dedicate this candle to break any hexes or curses that may be affecting me."

Candle Blessing:

Light the black candle and focus your attention on the flame.
Visualize the flame as a purifying and protective energy, capable of dispelling any negative influences.
Say the following incantation or create your own:
"Candle of black, with flickering light,
Break the hexes, dispel the blight.
Curses and spells, now be undone,
By the power of this candle, victory is won."

Crystal and Salt Activation:

Hold the amethyst or obsidian crystal in your hands and infuse it with your intention to break the hex or curse.

Sprinkle a small amount of salt into the dish or bowl, symbolizing purification and protection.

Writing Affirmations:

Take the small piece of paper and write down any specific hexes or curses you believe have been cast upon you.

Be clear and concise in your affirmations, focusing on breaking and releasing the negative energies.

For example, you could write, "I break any hexes or curses that have been sent my way. I am free from their influence."

Paper Charging:

Hold the piece of paper in your hands and visualize the negative energies being shattered and dissolved.

Visualize yourself surrounded by a protective shield of light, impenetrable to any harmful influences.

Hold the paper near the candle flame, allowing it to receive the energy of the flame and the intention you have set.

Burning and Cleansing:

Safely burn the small piece of paper using the candle flame, visualizing the hexes and curses being consumed by the fire.

As the paper burns, feel a sense of release and liberation from the negative energies that have been affecting you.

Allow the ashes to fall into the dish or bowl containing the salt, symbolizing the transmutation and purification of the energies.

Gratitude and Protection:

Express gratitude to the divine, the elements, and any spiritual guides or beings you work with for their assistance in breaking the hexes and curses.

Hold the amethyst or obsidian crystal in your hands and ask it to continue providing protection and purification.

Sprinkle a small amount of the salt around your living space or carry it with you as a protective talisman.

Closing:

Thank the elements and any spiritual guides or beings you invoked during the spell.
Blow out the candle, symbolizing the completion of the spell.
Dispose of the salt and ashes in a way that feels appropriate to you, such as burying them in the earth or dispersing them in flowing water.

Remember, this spell is a tool to help break negative energies and curses, but it is important to address the underlying causes and take action to protect yourself moving forward. Consider cleansing and protecting your energy regularly, practicing grounding and shielding techniques, and surrounding yourself with positive influences. Trust in your own inner strength and the power of the spell to assist you in breaking free from any hexes or curses that may have been affecting you.

Spell for Enhancing Spiritual Connection

Tools:

White candle
Amethyst or clear quartz crystal
Lavender incense or essential oil
A small dish or bowl
Pen or pencil
A small piece of paper

Instructions:

Preparation:

Find a quiet and sacred space where you can perform the spell without interruptions. Set up your altar or sacred space by placing the white candle, amethyst or clear quartz crystal, lavender incense or essential oil, dish or bowl, and a small piece of paper within reach.

Setting Intentions:

Close your eyes, take a few deep breaths, and center yourself.
Reflect on your intention for the spell, which is to enhance your spiritual connection and deepen your connection to the divine.

Candle Dedication:

Hold the white candle in your hands and visualize it as a beacon of divine light, symbolizing your spiritual connection.
State your intention clearly and strongly, such as "I dedicate this candle to enhance my spiritual connection and deepen my connection to the divine."

Candle Blessing:

Light the white candle and focus your attention on the flame.
Visualize the flame as a purifying and illuminating energy, inviting divine guidance and wisdom into your life.

Say the following incantation or create your own:

> "Candle of white, shining so bright,
> Enhance my spirit, expand my sight.
> Connection to divine, deepen and grow,
> Within the sacred, my spirit shall flow."

Crystal Activation:

Hold the amethyst or clear quartz crystal in your hands and infuse it with your intention to enhance your spiritual connection.
Visualize the crystal radiating a powerful, vibrant energy that aligns and harmonizes your spiritual self.

Incense or Essential Oil Ritual:

Light the lavender incense or use a few drops of lavender essential oil in a diffuser. Allow the aroma to fill the space and create a sense of calmness and tranquility, opening your senses to the spiritual realm.

Writing Affirmations:

Take the small piece of paper and write down affirmations that align with your intention of enhancing your spiritual connection.
Be clear and concise in your affirmations, focusing on the qualities you wish to embody and the experiences you desire.
For example, you could write, "I am deeply connected to the divine. My intuition is clear, and I receive guidance with ease."

Paper Charging:

Hold the piece of paper in your hands and visualize the affirmations becoming imprinted in your subconscious mind.
Feel the energy of the candle, crystal, and incense infusing the paper with their powerful vibrations.
Hold the paper near the candle flame, allowing it to receive the energy and light of the flame.

Burning and Release:

Safely burn the small piece of paper using the candle flame, visualizing your intentions being released into the universe.

As the paper burns, feel a sense of connection and alignment with the spiritual realm, knowing that your intentions have been heard and received.

Gratitude and Connection:

Express gratitude to the divine, the elements, and any spiritual guides or beings you work with for their assistance in enhancing your spiritual connection.

Hold the amethyst or clear quartz crystal in your hands and thank it for its support in deepening your connection to the spiritual realm.

Allow the candle to burn out completely, symbolizing the completion of the spell and the continuous presence of divine energy in your life.

Remember, this spell is a tool to assist you in enhancing your spiritual connection, but it is ultimately your own dedication, practice, and openness that will deepen your connection with the divine. Regularly engage in spiritual practices, such as meditation, prayer, and reflection, to nurture and strengthen your connection.

Spell for Strengthening Relationships

Tools:

Pink or red candle
Rose quartz crystal
Jasmine incense or essential oil
A small dish or bowl
Pen or pencil
A small piece of paper

Instructions:

Preparation:

Find a quiet and peaceful space where you can perform the spell without interruptions. Set up your altar or sacred space by placing the pink or red candle, rose quartz crystal, jasmine incense or essential oil, dish or bowl, and a small piece of paper within reach.

Setting Intentions:

Close your eyes, take a few deep breaths, and center yourself.
Reflect on your intention for the spell, which is to strengthen your relationships and cultivate love, harmony, and connection.

Candle Dedication:

Hold the pink or red candle in your hands and visualize it as a symbol of love and unity. State your intention clearly and strongly, such as "I dedicate this candle to strengthen my relationships, bringing love, harmony, and connection."

Candle Blessing:

Light the pink or red candle and focus your attention on the flame.
Visualize the flame as a warm and radiant energy that fills your space with love and positive vibrations.

Say the following incantation or create your own:

> "Candle of love, burning bright,
> Strengthen relationships day and night.

Harmony and connection, let it be,
Love and joy for all to see."

Crystal Activation:

Hold the rose quartz crystal in your hands and infuse it with your intention to strengthen your relationships.
Visualize the crystal emanating a gentle and loving energy, promoting understanding, forgiveness, and deep connection.

Incense or Essential Oil Ritual:

Light the jasmine incense or use a few drops of jasmine essential oil in a diffuser.
Allow the fragrance to fill the space, creating an atmosphere of love, attraction, and emotional harmony.

Writing Affirmations:

Take the small piece of paper and write down affirmations that support your intention of strengthening your relationships.
Be specific and heartfelt in your affirmations, focusing on qualities like love, understanding, trust, and open communication.
For example, you could write, "In my relationships, love flows freely. We communicate openly, trust deeply, and support one another unconditionally."

Paper Charging:

Hold the piece of paper in your hands and visualize the affirmations infusing it with love and positive energy.
Feel the energy of the candle, crystal, and incense permeating the paper, magnifying the power of your intentions.

Burning and Release:

Safely burn the small piece of paper using the candle flame, symbolizing the release of your intentions into the universe.
As the paper burns, envision your relationships growing stronger, filled with love, understanding, and harmony.

Gratitude and Connection:

Express gratitude to the divine, the elements, and any spiritual guides or beings you work with for their assistance in strengthening your relationships.
Hold the rose quartz crystal in your hands and thank it for its support in promoting love and harmony in your relationships.
Allow the candle to burn out completely, expressing gratitude for the energy and blessings it has provided.

Remember, this spell is a tool to assist you in strengthening your relationships, but it is your actions, communication, and genuine love and care that will nurture and sustain those connections. Use this spell as a reminder to continually invest in your relationships and foster a positive and loving environment.

Spell for Finding Lost Objects

Tools:

White candle
Clear quartz crystal
Lavender incense or essential oil
A small dish or bowl
Pen or pencil
A small piece of paper

Instructions:

Preparation:

Find a quiet and peaceful space where you can perform the spell without interruptions.
Set up your altar or sacred space by placing the white candle, clear quartz crystal, lavender incense or essential oil, dish or bowl, and a small piece of paper within reach.

Setting Intentions:

Close your eyes, take a few deep breaths, and center yourself.
Reflect on your intention for the spell, which is to find the lost object and retrieve it with ease and clarity.

Candle Dedication:

Hold the white candle in your hands and visualize it as a guiding light that will lead you to the lost object.
State your intention clearly and strongly, such as "I dedicate this candle to guide me in finding my lost object. May its light illuminate the path and help me locate it effortlessly."

Candle Blessing:

Light the white candle and focus your attention on the flame.
Visualize the flame as a powerful and illuminating energy that reveals the hidden location of the lost object.

Say the following incantation or create your own:

> "Candle of light, burn so bright,
> Guide me to my lost object, day or night.
> Show me the way, clear and true,
> Illuminate the path, help me find what is due."

Crystal Activation:

Hold the clear quartz crystal in your hands and infuse it with your intention to find the lost object.
Visualize the crystal emitting a vibrant and focused energy that enhances your intuition and perception.

Incense or Essential Oil Ritual:

Light the lavender incense or use a few drops of lavender essential oil in a diffuser.
Allow the soothing fragrance to fill the space, creating a calm and receptive atmosphere for your search.

Writing Description:

Take the small piece of paper and write a detailed description of the lost object.
Include any specific details, unique characteristics, or sentimental value associated with the object.
Visualize the object in your mind as you write, connecting with its energy.

Paper Charging:

Hold the piece of paper in your hands and imagine the description on the paper aligning with the energy of the lost object.
Feel a sense of connection and resonance between the paper and the object.

Focus and Meditation:

Close your eyes and hold the charged paper in your hands.
Visualize yourself moving through the space where the lost object may be, guided by the light of the candle and the energy of the crystal.
Trust your intuition and any impressions or images that come to mind, allowing them to guide you towards the object.

Gratitude and Release:

Express gratitude to the divine, the elements, and any spiritual guides or beings you work with for their assistance in finding the lost object.
Place the paper in the small dish or bowl and safely burn it using the candle flame, symbolizing the release of your intention into the universe.
As the paper burns, imagine the energy of your intention being sent out into the world, connecting with the energy of the lost object and guiding its return to you.

Remember, while this spell can assist in finding lost objects, it is essential to remain open, observant, and actively search for the object in practical ways. The spell serves as a support to enhance your intuition and increase your chances of locating the lost item. Trust your instincts and be patient as you follow any leads or signs that may arise during your search.

Spell for Overcoming Obstacles

Tools:

Yellow candle
Tiger's eye crystal
Sandalwood incense or essential oil
A small dish or bowl
Pen or pencil
A small piece of paper

Instructions:

Preparation:

Find a quiet and peaceful space where you can perform the spell without interruptions. Set up your altar or sacred space by placing the yellow candle, tiger's eye crystal, sandalwood incense or essential oil, dish or bowl, and a small piece of paper within reach.

Setting Intentions:

Close your eyes, take a few deep breaths, and center yourself.
Reflect on the specific obstacle or challenge you are facing and your intention to overcome it with strength and determination.

Candle Dedication:

Hold the yellow candle in your hands and visualize it as a symbol of energy and motivation to overcome obstacles.
State your intention clearly and strongly, such as "I dedicate this candle to empower me in overcoming the obstacle before me. May its light illuminate the path and grant me the strength to overcome."

Candle Blessing:

Light the yellow candle and focus your attention on the flame.
Visualize the flame as a source of courage and resilience, burning away the obstacles that stand in your way.

Say the following incantation or create your own:

> "Candle of yellow, shining bright,
> Fill me with strength and inner light.
> Clear my path, obstacles be gone,
> Empower me to overcome and move on."

Crystal Activation:

Hold the tiger's eye crystal in your hands and envision it radiating a powerful and protective energy.
Feel the crystal's energy merging with your own, providing you with strength and confidence.

Incense or Essential Oil Ritual:

Light the sandalwood incense or use a few drops of sandalwood essential oil in a diffuser.
Allow the comforting and grounding aroma to fill the space, creating a sense of stability and focus.

Writing Affirmations:

Take the small piece of paper and write down positive affirmations related to overcoming obstacles.
Use affirmative statements such as "I am strong and capable," "I am resilient in the face of challenges," or any other affirmations that resonate with you.
Paper Charging:

Hold the piece of paper in your hands and visualize the affirmations on the paper aligning with your energy and mindset.
Feel a sense of empowerment and determination as you connect with the affirmations.

Focus and Meditation:

Close your eyes and hold the charged paper in your hands.
Visualize yourself confidently and skillfully navigating through the obstacles in your path.
Envision the barriers diminishing and transforming into opportunities for growth and success.

Gratitude and Release:

Express gratitude to the divine, the elements, and any spiritual guides or beings you work with for their assistance in overcoming obstacles.

Place the paper in the small dish or bowl and safely burn it using the candle flame, symbolizing the release of your intentions into the universe.

As the paper burns, imagine the energy of your intentions spreading out into the world, clearing the way for your success.

Remember, while this spell can assist in overcoming obstacles, it is essential to take practical actions and make proactive efforts to address the challenges you face. The spell serves as a support to strengthen your resolve and provide you with the necessary energy and mindset to overcome the obstacles in your path. Trust in your abilities and remain determined as you navigate through any difficulties.

Spell for Enhancing Creativity and Inspiration

Tools:

Purple candle
Amethyst crystal
Lavender incense or essential oil
A small dish or bowl
Pen or pencil
A blank sheet of paper
Instructions:

Preparation:

Find a quiet and comfortable space where you can focus your energy and creativity.
Set up your altar or sacred space by placing the purple candle, amethyst crystal, lavender incense or essential oil, dish or bowl, and a blank sheet of paper within reach.

Setting Intentions:

Close your eyes, take a few deep breaths, and center yourself.
Reflect on your desire to enhance your creativity and invite inspiration into your life.

Candle Dedication:

Hold the purple candle in your hands and visualize it as a symbol of creative energy and inspiration.
State your intention clearly and strongly, such as "I dedicate this candle to awaken and amplify my creative abilities. May its flame ignite my imagination and bring forth inspiration."

Candle Blessing:

Light the purple candle and focus your attention on the flame.
Visualize the flame as a source of creative energy, burning away any blockages or limitations that hinder your inspiration.

Say the following incantation or create your own:

> "Purple candle, burning bright,
> Ignite my creativity with your light.

Let inspiration flow, let ideas soar,
My creative spirit forevermore."

Crystal Activation:

Hold the amethyst crystal in your hands and envision it radiating a vibrant and stimulating energy.
Feel the crystal's energy merging with your own, expanding your creative capacity.

Incense or Essential Oil Ritual:

Light the lavender incense or use a few drops of lavender essential oil in a diffuser.
Allow the calming and soothing aroma to fill the space, creating an atmosphere conducive to inspiration and creative flow.

Writing Affirmations:

Take the blank sheet of paper and write down positive affirmations related to creativity and inspiration.
Use affirmative statements such as "I am a vessel of creative energy," "Inspiration flows effortlessly through me," or any other affirmations that resonate with you.

Paper Charging:

Hold the paper in your hands and visualize the affirmations on the paper aligning with your creative essence.
Feel a sense of excitement and passion as you connect with the affirmations.

Focus and Meditation:

Close your eyes and hold the charged paper in your hands.
Visualize yourself immersed in a vibrant, colorful world of creativity and inspiration.
See yourself engaging in your creative pursuits with enthusiasm and confidence, effortlessly bringing your ideas to life.

Gratitude and Release:

Express gratitude to the divine, the elements, and any spiritual guides or beings you work with for their assistance in enhancing your creativity and inspiration.
Place the paper in the small dish or bowl, and using the candle flame, safely burn it, symbolizing the release of your intentions into the universe.

As the paper burns, imagine your intentions being carried on the winds, connecting with the cosmic energy of creativity and inspiration.

Remember, while this spell can enhance your creativity and inspiration, it is important to actively engage in creative practices and nurture your creative spirit. The spell serves as a catalyst and reminder of your innate creative abilities. Allow yourself to be open to inspiration, trust your intuition, and embrace the joy of expressing your unique creativity in the world.

Spell for Banishing Nightmares and Bad Dreams

Tools:

White candle
Amethyst crystal
Lavender incense or essential oil
Small bowl of water
Pen or pencil
A small piece of paper
Protective herbs (such as lavender, rosemary, or chamomile)

Instructions:

Preparation:

Find a quiet and comfortable space where you can focus your energy and intention.
Set up your altar or sacred space by placing the white candle, amethyst crystal, lavender incense or essential oil, small bowl of water, pen or pencil, and the small piece of paper within reach.
Optionally, have the protective herbs nearby for later use.

Cleansing and Grounding:

Take a moment to ground yourself by taking several deep breaths and focusing on your intention to banish nightmares and bad dreams.
Light the lavender incense or use a few drops of lavender essential oil in a diffuser to cleanse the space and create a calming atmosphere.

Candle Dedication:

Hold the white candle in your hands and visualize it as a symbol of divine light and protection.
State your intention clearly and strongly, such as "I dedicate this candle to banish nightmares and bad dreams. May its flame dispel darkness and bring peaceful sleep."

Candle Blessing:

Light the white candle and focus your attention on the flame.
Visualize the flame growing brighter and filling the space with pure, radiant light.

Say the following incantation or create your own:

> "Candle of white, shining so bright,
> Banish the nightmares, bring peaceful night.
> With divine light, protect my sleep,
> May rest and tranquility be mine to keep."

Crystal Activation:

Hold the amethyst crystal in your hands and visualize it absorbing any negative energies associated with nightmares and bad dreams.
See the crystal radiating a soothing and protective energy.

Water Purification:

Dip your fingertips into the bowl of water.
Close your eyes and envision the water becoming infused with divine healing energy.
Sprinkle a few drops of the water around your sleeping area or on your pillow, saying:
"With this blessed water, I cleanse and purify,
Driving away darkness, bringing peace nearby.
As I sleep, protect me from all that may harm,
Sweet dreams and serenity, now be my charm."

Writing Affirmation:

Take the small piece of paper and write down a positive affirmation or intention related to peaceful sleep and freedom from nightmares.
For example, you can write, "I sleep peacefully and am free from nightmares," or any other statement that resonates with you.

Paper Folding:

Fold the paper neatly, symbolizing the containment and sealing of your intention.
You can fold it once or multiple times, whatever feels right to you.

Protective Herb Placement (optional):

If you have protective herbs, sprinkle a small amount of the herbs around your sleeping area or tuck them under your pillow.
Visualize the herbs creating a protective barrier against negative energies.

Final Affirmation and Release:

Hold the folded paper in your hands and close your eyes.
Focus on the intention written on the paper and feel the energy of peaceful sleep and freedom from nightmares.
State your affirmation aloud or silently, infusing it with belief and conviction.
When ready, place the folded paper near the candle flame, allowing it to catch fire and burn completely in a fire-safe container.
As the paper burns, visualize the release of your intention into the universe, knowing that it is manifesting and bringing about the desired changes.

Remember, while this spell can aid in banishing nightmares and bad dreams, it is also essential to establish a calming bedtime routine and create a sleep-friendly environment. Practice relaxation techniques, ensure a comfortable sleeping space, and cultivate a sense of peace before sleep. Trust in the power of the spell and your own ability to manifest peaceful sleep and pleasant dreams.

Spell for Finding Inner Peace and Serenity

Tools:

Blue or purple candle
Clear quartz crystal
Lavender incense or essential oil
Small bowl of water
Pen or pencil
A small piece of paper
Optional: calming herbs (such as chamomile or lavender)

Instructions:

Preparation:

Find a quiet and peaceful space where you can focus your energy and intention.
Set up your altar or sacred space by placing the blue or purple candle, clear quartz crystal, lavender incense or essential oil, small bowl of water, pen or pencil, and the small piece of paper within reach.
Optionally, have the calming herbs nearby for later use.

Cleansing and Grounding:

Take a few moments to ground yourself by taking deep breaths and centering your energy.
Light the lavender incense or use a few drops of lavender essential oil in a diffuser to cleanse the space and create a calming atmosphere.

Candle Dedication:

Hold the blue or purple candle in your hands and envision it as a source of inner peace and serenity.
State your intention clearly and strongly, such as "I dedicate this candle to find inner peace and invite serenity into my life. May its flame illuminate the path to tranquility."

Candle Blessing:

Light the blue or purple candle and focus your attention on the flame.
Visualize the flame growing brighter, radiating a soothing and peaceful energy.

Say the following incantation or create your own:

"Candle of blue/purple, light so serene,
Bring me inner peace, calm and serene.
With each gentle flicker, my soul finds rest,
Serenity and harmony, I am blessed."

Crystal Activation:

Hold the clear quartz crystal in your hands and envision it as a vessel of pure and clear energy.
Feel its vibrations resonating with your intention for inner peace and serenity.
Place the crystal near the lit candle or hold it throughout the spell to amplify the energy.

Water Purification:

Dip your fingertips into the bowl of water.
Close your eyes and imagine the water being infused with tranquil and healing energy.
Sprinkle a few drops of the water on your forehead, saying:
"Water pure, wash away distress,
Calm my mind, bring me peacefulness.
As I seek serenity within my core,
May inner peace and tranquility restore."

Writing Affirmation:

Take the small piece of paper and write down a positive affirmation or intention related to finding inner peace and serenity.
For example, you can write, "I am at peace, and serenity fills my being," or any other statement that resonates with you.

Paper Folding:

Fold the paper neatly, symbolizing the containment and sealing of your intention.
You can fold it once or multiple times, whatever feels right to you.

Optional: Calming Herb Placement:

If you have chosen calming herbs, scatter a small amount around your sacred space or place them near the candle and crystal.
Visualize their calming and soothing properties enveloping the space and enhancing the spell's effectiveness.

Final Affirmation and Release:

Hold the folded paper in your hands and close your eyes.
Focus on the intention written on the paper and feel the energy of inner peace and serenity flowing through you.
State your affirmation aloud or silently, infusing it with belief and conviction.
When ready, place the folded paper near the candle flame, allowing it to catch fire and burn completely in a fire-safe container.
As the paper burns, visualize your intention being released into the universe, trusting that it will manifest in your life.

Closing:

Express gratitude to the elements, the candle, crystal, water, and any other tools or beings you called upon during the spell.
Extinguish the candle, and if desired, keep the crystal in a safe place as a reminder of your intention and the energy of inner peace and serenity.

Remember, spells are a means to focus and direct your intentions, but ultimately, the true power lies within you. Cultivate a mindset of peace, practice self-care, and embrace mindful practices to enhance your journey toward inner peace and serenity.

Spell for Enhancing Spiritual Vision

Tools:

Purple candle
Amethyst crystal
Frankincense incense or essential oil
Small mirror or reflective surface
Pen or pencil
White paper
Optional: third eye symbol or image

Instructions:

Preparation:

Find a quiet and sacred space where you can perform the spell without interruption.
Set up your altar or sacred space by placing the purple candle, amethyst crystal, frankincense incense or essential oil, small mirror, pen or pencil, and white paper within reach.
Optionally, have a third eye symbol or image nearby to focus your intention.

Cleansing and Grounding:

Take a few deep breaths to center yourself and clear your mind.
Light the frankincense incense or use a few drops of frankincense essential oil in a diffuser to cleanse the space and create a sacred atmosphere.

Candle Dedication:

Hold the purple candle in your hands and visualize it as a beacon of spiritual illumination.
State your intention clearly and firmly, such as "I dedicate this candle to enhance my spiritual vision and awaken my inner sight. May its flame guide me to higher realms of knowledge and insight."

Candle Blessing:

Light the purple candle and focus your attention on the flame.
Visualize the flame growing brighter and more vibrant, radiating a powerful and illuminating energy.

Say the following incantation or create your own:

> "Candle of purple, flame of insight,
> Illuminate my path, enhance my sight.
> Awaken the wisdom deep within,
> Spiritual vision, let it begin."

Crystal Activation:

Hold the amethyst crystal in your hands and connect with its energy.
Envision the crystal as a conduit for spiritual insight and clarity.
Place the crystal near the lit candle or hold it throughout the spell to amplify the energy.

Mirror Reflection:

Take the small mirror or reflective surface and place it in front of you.
Gaze into the mirror, focusing on your own eyes and the reflection of your inner self.
Allow yourself to be open and receptive to any insights or messages that may come through.

Affirmation and Intention:

Take the pen or pencil and the white paper.
Write down a statement of intention related to enhancing your spiritual vision.
For example, you can write, "I see clearly with my spiritual eyes, guided by divine wisdom and insight."

Symbolic Representation:

If you have a third eye symbol or image, hold it in your hand or place it near the mirror.
Visualize the symbol activating and opening your third eye, the center of spiritual vision and intuition.

Affirmation and Activation:

Read your written intention aloud or silently, infusing it with belief and conviction.
Hold the paper close to your heart and say:

> "With this spell, my vision is enhanced,
> My spiritual sight is awakened and advanced.
> Through divine guidance and inner knowing,
> I see beyond, my insight is growing."

Reflection and Meditation:

Return your gaze to the mirror, looking into your own eyes.
Allow any insights, visions, or intuitive messages to come forward.
Stay in this reflective state for as long as feels comfortable, embracing the energy of enhanced spiritual vision.

Closing:

Express gratitude to the elements, the candle, crystal, mirror, and any other tools or beings you called upon during the spell.
Extinguish the candle and keep the paper with your intention in a safe place or carry it with you as a reminder of your commitment to enhancing your spiritual vision.

Remember, spells are a means to focus and direct your intentions, but the true power lies within you. Regular spiritual practices, such as meditation, energy work, and connecting with nature, can further enhance and develop your spiritual vision. Trust in your intuition and embrace the journey of deepening your connection with the spiritual realms.

Spell for Harmonizing Relationships

Tools:

Pink or green candle (pink for romantic relationships, green for general relationships)
Rose quartz crystal
Jasmine incense or essential oil
Small bowl of water
Pen or pencil
White paper
Optional: a photo or representation of the person(s) involved in the relationship
Instructions:

Preparation:

Find a peaceful and undisturbed space to perform the spell.
Set up your altar or sacred space with the pink or green candle, rose quartz crystal, jasmine incense or essential oil, small bowl of water, pen or pencil, and white paper.
If you have a photo or representation of the person(s) involved in the relationship, place it on the altar.
Cleansing and Grounding:

Take a moment to center yourself and release any distractions or negative energies.
Light the jasmine incense or use a few drops of jasmine essential oil in a diffuser to purify the space and create a harmonious atmosphere.
Candle Dedication:

Hold the pink or green candle in your hands and visualize it as a symbol of love, harmony, and unity.
State your intention clearly and firmly, such as "I dedicate this candle to harmonize and strengthen the relationship between [names of the individuals]. May it be filled with love, understanding, and mutual support."
Candle Blessing:

Light the candle and focus your attention on the flame.
Visualize the flame radiating warmth, love, and positive energy, enveloping the relationship with its gentle glow.
Say the following incantation or create your own:
"Candle of harmony, burn bright and true,
Bring love and unity, make the bond renew.
In this relationship, let conflicts cease,

May harmony and joy fill every crease."

Crystal Activation:

Hold the rose quartz crystal in your hands and connect with its loving and gentle energy. Envision the crystal infusing the relationship with unconditional love, understanding, and compassion.
Place the crystal near the candle to amplify its energy throughout the spell.
Water Cleansing:

Take the small bowl of water and hold it in your hands.
Visualize the water as a purifying and healing force, capable of washing away any negative energies or misunderstandings within the relationship.
Gently sprinkle or dip your fingers into the water, symbolizing the cleansing and purifying of the relationship.
Affirmation and Intention:

Take the pen or pencil and the white paper.
Write down your intention for the harmonization of the relationship, focusing on qualities like love, understanding, respect, and compromise.
For example, you can write, "In this relationship, we communicate with kindness and empathy, resolving conflicts with love and understanding."
Visualization:

Visualize the individuals involved in the relationship, including yourself, surrounded by a soft, pink or green glow of harmonious energy.
See them communicating openly and honestly, expressing their feelings with love and respect.
Imagine any past conflicts or misunderstandings dissolving, replaced by a deep sense of unity and harmony.
Affirmation and Activation:

Read your written intention aloud or silently, infusing it with belief and positive energy.
Hold the paper close to your heart and say:
"By the power of love and divine grace,
I harmonize this relationship, every trace.
May understanding and unity be our guide,
Love and harmony forever reside."

Water Blessing:

Take a few drops of the blessed water and sprinkle it gently around the candle and altar as a symbolic blessing of the relationship.
Feel the purifying and harmonizing energy permeating the space.
Gratitude and Closing:

Express gratitude to the divine or higher power for the blessings bestowed upon the relationship.
Thank the elements and tools used in the spell for their assistance.
Blow out the candle, knowing that the energy of love and harmony will continue to work in the relationship.
Remember, a spell is a focused intention combined with ritual actions. Trust in the power of your intention and the energy you put into the spell. Keep an open heart, communicate honestly, and embrace the path of harmony and unity in your relationships.

Spell for Protection Against Psychic Attacks

Tools:

Black candle
Amethyst crystal
Frankincense incense or essential oil
Small bowl of salt
White sage bundle or palo santo stick

Instructions:

Preparation:

Find a quiet and undisturbed space where you can perform the spell.
Set up your altar or sacred space with the black candle, amethyst crystal, frankincense incense or essential oil, small bowl of salt, and white sage bundle or palo santo stick.

Cleansing and Grounding:

Begin by cleansing yourself and the space. Light the white sage bundle or palo santo stick and pass it around your body, allowing the smoke to purify your energy field. Then, move around the room, focusing on the corners and areas where negative energy may linger.
Take a few deep breaths, grounding yourself and releasing any tension or stress.

Candle Dedication:

Hold the black candle in your hands and envision it as a shield of protection against psychic attacks.
State your intention clearly and firmly, such as "I dedicate this candle to safeguard and shield me from any negative or harmful psychic energies. May it create a barrier of protection around me."

Candle Blessing:

Light the black candle and focus your attention on the flame.
Visualize the flame growing stronger and brighter, forming a protective shield around you.

Say the following incantation or create your own:

> "Candle of darkness, burning bright,
> Protect me from harm with your ancient might.
> Shield my mind, my spirit, my soul,
> Ward off all psychic attacks and make me whole."

Crystal Activation:

Hold the amethyst crystal in your hands and connect with its calming and protective energy.
Envision the crystal radiating a purple light that surrounds and fortifies your aura, forming an impenetrable barrier against negative psychic energies.
Place the crystal near the candle to enhance its protective properties.

Incense Invocation:

Light the frankincense incense or use a few drops of frankincense essential oil in a diffuser.
As the smoke rises, imagine it forming a protective shield around you, repelling any negative or harmful psychic influences.

State the following invocation or create your own:

> "By the power of sacred smoke and scent,
> I invoke protection, a psychic shield to prevent.
> Let no harm or ill intent pass through,
> Only love and light remain true."

Salt Purification:

Take a pinch of salt from the small bowl and sprinkle it around your sacred space.
Visualize the salt forming a protective boundary, purifying and repelling any negative energies.
Affirm that only positive and beneficial energies may enter your space.

Affirmation and Intent:

Close your eyes and focus on your intention to protect yourself from psychic attacks.

Repeat the following affirmation or create your own:

> "I am shielded, I am strong,
> Protected from all that's wrong.
> My psychic boundaries are firm and secure,
> No negative energy can endure."

Visualize the Shield:

Visualize a shimmering shield of protective energy surrounding you, extending from the top of your head to the soles of your feet.
See this shield as impenetrable, blocking and deflecting any negative or harmful psychic energies that may come your way.

Gratitude and Closing:

Express gratitude to the divine or higher power for providing protection and guidance.
Thank the elements and tools used in the spell for their assistance.
Allow the candle to burn out safely or snuff it out with the intention of keeping the protective energy intact.
Safely extinguish the incense and dispose of the ashes.
Store the amethyst crystal in a safe place and recharge it periodically to maintain its protective properties.

Remember, the power of this spell lies in your intention and focus. Trust in your ability to protect yourself and maintain a positive and empowered mindset. Regularly reinforce your intention for protection and perform the spell as needed to keep your psychic boundaries strong and secure.

Spell for Finding Lost Love

Tools:

Pink candle
Rose quartz crystal
Jasmine incense or essential oil
Small piece of paper
Pen or marker

Instructions:

Preparation:

Find a quiet and undisturbed space where you can perform the spell.
Set up your altar or sacred space with the pink candle, rose quartz crystal, jasmine incense or essential oil, small piece of paper, and pen or marker.

Candle Dedication:

Hold the pink candle in your hands and envision it as a beacon of love, drawing your lost love back to you.
State your intention clearly and firmly, such as "I dedicate this candle to the purpose of finding and reuniting with my lost love. May it guide and attract love back into my life."

Candle Blessing:

Light the pink candle and focus your attention on the flame.
Visualize the flame as a powerful magnet, pulling love and romance towards you.

Say the following incantation or create your own:

> "Candle of love, burning bright,
> Bring back to me my heart's delight.
> Guide my lost love, let our paths align,
> Rekindle the passion, let true love shine."

Crystal Activation:

Hold the rose quartz crystal in your hands and connect with its gentle and loving energy.

Envision the crystal emanating a warm and inviting glow, attracting the love and affection of your lost love.
Place the crystal near the candle to amplify its magnetic properties.

Incense Invocation:

Light the jasmine incense or use a few drops of jasmine essential oil in a diffuser.
As the sweet aroma fills the air, imagine it spreading a captivating fragrance that entices your lost love to return.

State the following invocation or create your own:

> "With the scent of jasmine in the air,
> I beckon my lost love, with love and care.
> Let our hearts reconnect and our love ignite,
> Across time and space, may our love reunite."

Write Your Desire:

Take the small piece of paper and write down your desire to find your lost love.
Be specific and heartfelt in expressing your intentions and the qualities of the love you wish to rekindle.
Fold the paper neatly and hold it in your hands, infusing it with your energy and intention.

Affirmation and Intent:

Close your eyes and hold the folded paper against your heart.
Repeat the following affirmation or create your own:
"I call upon the universe's power and grace,
To guide my lost love back to this place.
With pure intentions and an open heart,
I manifest the reunion, a fresh new start."

Visualize the Reunion:

Visualize yourself and your lost love reuniting in a loving and harmonious embrace.
Feel the joy, love, and connection as if it is already happening in the present moment.
Hold this image in your mind, allowing it to fill you with hope and anticipation.
Release and Surrender:

Burn the folded paper with your desire safely in a fireproof container.
As it burns, release your attachment to the outcome and surrender your desires to the universe, trusting that what is meant to be will manifest.

Gratitude and Closing:

Express gratitude to the divine or higher power for guiding and supporting your intentions.
Thank the elements and tools used in the spell for their assistance.
Allow the candle to burn out safely or snuff it out with the intention of keeping the love energy alive.
Safely extinguish the incense and dispose of the ashes.

Remember, while spells can be helpful in focusing your intentions and energy, they are not a guarantee of specific outcomes. It's essential to have an open mind and be receptive to the opportunities and possibilities that come your way. Stay open to love and trust the journey of finding your lost love.

Spell for Opening Pathways to Success

Tools:

Yellow candle
Citrine crystal
Patchouli incense or essential oil
Small piece of paper
Pen or marker

Instructions:

Preparation:

Find a quiet and undisturbed space where you can perform the spell.
Set up your altar or sacred space with the yellow candle, citrine crystal, patchouli incense or essential oil, small piece of paper, and pen or marker.

Candle Dedication:

Hold the yellow candle in your hands and visualize it as a source of bright, vibrant energy that attracts success and opportunities.
State your intention clearly and confidently, such as "I dedicate this candle to the purpose of opening pathways to success in my life. May it illuminate my way and bring forth abundant opportunities."

Candle Blessing:

Light the yellow candle and focus your attention on the flame.
Imagine the flame as a guiding light, illuminating the path to success and abundance.

Recite the following incantation or create your own:

> "Candle of yellow, burning bright,
> Open the pathways to success and light.
> Guide me on my journey, help me see,
> Opportunities and abundance that await me."

Crystal Activation:

Hold the citrine crystal in your hands and connect with its vibrant and empowering energy.
Visualize the crystal radiating a golden glow, infusing you with confidence, motivation, and the ability to seize opportunities.
Place the crystal near the candle to amplify its energies.

Incense Invocation:

Light the patchouli incense or use a few drops of patchouli essential oil in a diffuser.
As the rich aroma fills the air, feel its grounding and uplifting properties enhancing your focus and determination.

State the following invocation or create your own:

> "With the scent of patchouli, I invoke,
> Success and abundance, let them evoke.
> Clear my mind, grant me clarity,
> Open the pathways, so success finds me."

Write Your Goals:

Take the small piece of paper and write down your goals and aspirations for success.
Be specific and detailed in describing what you wish to achieve and the steps you will take to get there.
Fold the paper neatly and hold it in your hands, infusing it with your energy and determination.

Affirmation and Intent:

Close your eyes and hold the folded paper against your heart.

Repeat the following affirmation or create your own:

> "I call upon the universe's guiding light,
> To open pathways, success shining bright.
> With focus and determination, I shall proceed,
> Opportunities arise, fulfilling my every need."

Visualize the Pathways:

Visualize yourself standing at the beginning of a path, with success and abundance stretching out before you.
See yourself walking confidently along this path, encountering opportunities and achieving your goals.
Hold this image in your mind, allowing it to inspire and motivate you.
\
Release and Surrender:

Burn the folded paper with your goals safely in a fireproof container.
As it burns, release any doubts, fears, or limitations that may hinder your path to success.
Surrender your desires to the universe, trusting that the right opportunities will come your way.

Gratitude and Closing:

Express gratitude to the divine or higher power for guiding and supporting your intentions.
Thank the elements and tools used in the spell for their assistance.
Allow the candle to burn out safely or snuff it out with the intention of keeping the pathway to success illuminated.
Carry the citrine crystal with you or keep it in a prominent place as a reminder of your goals and intentions.

Remember, this spell is a tool to align your energy and focus your intentions. It is essential to take inspired actions, remain proactive, and seize opportunities that come your way. Trust in the process and believe in your ability to manifest success in your life.

Spell for Releasing Karmic Patterns

Tools:

White candle
Clear quartz crystal
Frankincense incense or essential oil
Small piece of paper
Pen or marker
Instructions:

Preparation:

Find a quiet and peaceful space where you can perform the spell without interruptions. Set up your altar or sacred space with the white candle, clear quartz crystal, frankincense incense or essential oil, small piece of paper, and pen or marker.

Candle Dedication:

Hold the white candle in your hands and visualize it as a symbol of purity and divine light.
State your intention clearly and confidently, such as "I dedicate this candle to the purpose of releasing karmic patterns that no longer serve me. May its flame illuminate my path to freedom and transformation."

Candle Blessing:

Light the white candle and focus your attention on the flame.
Visualize the flame as a purifying and transformative energy that burns away karmic ties and patterns.

Recite the following incantation or create your own:

> "Candle of white, shining bright,
> Release me from karmic ties tonight.
> Burn away patterns that hold me down,
> Grant me freedom, my spirit unbound."

Crystal Activation:

Hold the clear quartz crystal in your hands and connect with its cleansing and amplifying properties.
Visualize the crystal absorbing and transmuting any stagnant or negative energies associated with your karmic patterns.
Place the crystal near the candle to enhance its energy and assist in the release process.

Incense Invocation:

Light the frankincense incense or use a few drops of frankincense essential oil in a diffuser.
As the sacred smoke rises, envision it purifying your energy field and creating a sacred space for transformation.

State the following invocation or create your own:

> "With the scent of frankincense, I call,
> Release karmic patterns, large and small.
> Purify my spirit, clear and bright,
> Transforming darkness into pure light."

Write Your Intentions:

Take the small piece of paper and write down the karmic patterns or behaviors you wish to release.
Be specific and honest in describing the patterns that no longer serve your highest good.
Fold the paper neatly and hold it in your hands, infusing it with your intention to release these patterns.

Affirmation and Intent:

Close your eyes and hold the folded paper against your heart.

Repeat the following affirmation or create your own:

> "I release karmic patterns that bind,
> Embracing freedom and peace of mind.
> With clarity and strength, I now break free,
> Transforming my destiny, so mote it be."

Visualize the Release:

Visualize the paper with your written intentions dissolving into pure light.
See the energy of the karmic patterns being released and transformed into positive, empowering energy.
Hold this image in your mind, allowing a sense of liberation and relief to wash over you.

Burning and Release:

Safely burn the folded paper with your intentions in a fireproof container.
As it burns, imagine the release of the karmic patterns and feel the weight lifted from your being.
Let go of any attachments or emotional ties associated with those patterns, knowing that you are freeing yourself.

Gratitude and Closing:

Express gratitude to the divine or higher power for guiding and supporting your intentions.
Thank the elements and tools used in the spell for their assistance.
Allow the candle to burn out completely or extinguish it with gratitude when you're ready to close the ritual.

Remember, this spell is a catalyst for change, but true transformation comes through self-reflection, personal growth, and conscious choices. Take inspired action and continue to release and heal any remnants of karmic patterns as you move forward on your journey.

Spell for Cleansing and Blessing Sacred Objects

Tools:

Sacred object(s) to be cleansed and blessed
White sage bundle or palo santo stick
Bowl of purified water
Salt (preferably sea salt)
Small white cloth or altar cloth
Instructions:

Preparation:

Find a quiet and sacred space where you can perform the spell without interruptions.
Set up your altar or sacred space with the white sage bundle or palo santo stick, bowl of purified water, salt, and small white cloth or altar cloth.

Setting the Intention:

Hold the sacred object(s) in your hands and connect with their energy.
Set a clear intention to cleanse and bless the object(s), infusing them with positive and sacred vibrations.

Purification with Smoke:

Light the white sage bundle or palo santo stick and allow the smoke to billow.
Pass the sacred object(s) through the smoke, allowing the fragrant smoke to cleanse and purify them.
Visualize any negative or stagnant energies being released and replaced with pure and positive vibrations.

Cleansing with Water:

Dip your fingers into the bowl of purified water and sprinkle a few drops over the sacred object(s).
As you do so, visualize the water washing away any impurities or energetic debris from the object(s).
Imagine the water restoring the object(s) to their original, pure state.

Blessing with Salt:

Take a small pinch of salt and sprinkle it over the sacred object(s) in a circular motion.

While doing this, recite the following incantation or create your own:

> "By the power of Earth and Sea,
> I cleanse and bless this object, thee.
> Negativity be gone, replaced by light,
> A sacred tool, divinely bright."

Placement on Altar Cloth:

Lay the cleansed and blessed object(s) on the small white cloth or altar cloth.
This cloth acts as a sacred space for the object(s) and helps maintain their positive energy.

Gratitude and Closing:

Express gratitude to the divine or higher power for their presence and assistance in the cleansing and blessing.
Thank the elements of fire, water, earth, and air for their purifying and sacred energies.
Leave the object(s) on the altar cloth for a designated period, allowing them to absorb the positive vibrations of the space.

Note: It's important to trust your intuition when performing this spell. You can modify it according to your beliefs and personal practices. Remember, the cleansing and blessing of sacred objects is a sacred act that connects you with the spiritual realm and enhances the object's energy for its intended purpose.

Spell for Enhancing Intuition and Clarity

Tools:

Amethyst crystal
White candle
Lavender incense
Small bowl of purified water
Pen and paper

Instructions:

Preparation:

Find a quiet and comfortable space where you can perform the spell without distractions. Set up your altar or sacred space with the amethyst crystal, white candle, lavender incense, small bowl of purified water, and pen and paper.

Grounding and Centering:

Sit in a comfortable position and take a few deep breaths to center yourself.
Close your eyes and visualize roots extending from your feet, grounding you to the Earth.
Feel your connection with the Earth's energy, drawing strength and stability from it.

Lighting the Candle:

Light the white candle, representing clarity and illumination.

As you do so, recite the following incantation or create your own:

> "By the flame's pure light so bright,
> I awaken my intuition's sight.
> Grant me clarity, insight so keen,
> May my intuition guide and be seen."

Cleansing with Incense:

Light the lavender incense, known for its calming and clarifying properties.
Pass the amethyst crystal through the smoke, allowing the aroma to cleanse and purify its energy.

Visualize the smoke removing any blockages or distractions, leaving the crystal and your mind clear and receptive.

Activation with Water:

Dip your fingers into the small bowl of purified water.
Gently sprinkle a few droplets of water onto the amethyst crystal.
As you do so, visualize the water activating the crystal's intuitive powers and enhancing its ability to amplify your own intuition.

Written Intention:

Take the pen and paper and write down your intention for enhanced intuition and clarity.
Be specific about the areas of your life where you seek guidance and insight.
Use empowering language and affirmations to reinforce your intention.

Focus and Meditation:

Hold the amethyst crystal in your hands, close your eyes, and take a few deep breaths.
Visualize the energy of the crystal merging with your own energy, creating a harmonious and powerful connection.
Allow yourself to enter a meditative state, focusing on your breath and opening yourself to receive intuitive messages and insights.

Closing and Gratitude:

Express gratitude to the divine or higher power for their guidance and assistance in enhancing your intuition and clarity.
Blow out the white candle, symbolizing the completion of the spell.
Keep the amethyst crystal with you or in a sacred space as a reminder of your intention and a tool for enhancing intuition.

Note: This spell is a personal and introspective practice. Trust your intuition and adapt the instructions and incantation to resonate with your beliefs and intentions. Remember to approach the spell with sincerity, respect, and a genuine desire to enhance your intuition and clarity.

Spell for Healing Ancestral Lineage

Tools:

A small bowl or dish
Fresh or dried herbs (such as sage, rosemary, or lavender)
A white candle
A lighter or matches
Pen and paper

Instructions:

Preparation:

Find a quiet and peaceful space where you can perform the spell without distractions. Set up your altar or sacred space with the small bowl or dish, herbs, white candle, lighter or matches, and pen and paper.

Grounding and Centering:

Take a few deep breaths to calm your mind and focus your energy.
Visualize yourself rooted to the earth, feeling connected and grounded.

Lighting the Candle:

Light the white candle, representing purity, healing, and connection to the divine.

As you light the candle, say the following incantation or create your own:

> "By the light of this sacred flame,
> I call upon ancestral healing's name.
> With love and respect, I now reclaim
> The power to heal our ancestral pain."

Herbal Cleansing:

Take a handful of the herbs and place them into the small bowl or dish.
Light the herbs using the flame of the candle, allowing them to smolder and release their aromatic smoke.
Waft the smoke around your body and over the ancestral objects or photographs, visualizing the smoke purifying and healing any ancestral wounds or negative energy.

Invocation and Prayer:

Hold the pen and paper in your hands, close your eyes, and take a moment to connect with your ancestors.
Speak from your heart and invoke the presence of your ancestors, expressing your desire for healing and transformation within your ancestral lineage.
Ask for their guidance, love, and support in this healing journey.
Write down a prayer or affirmation on the paper, expressing your intention for healing and releasing any ancestral burdens.

Offering and Release:

Tear the paper with your written prayer or affirmation into small pieces.
Hold the torn paper in your hands and offer it to the flame of the candle, visualizing the release of any negative ancestral patterns or wounds.
As the paper burns, imagine the energy transforming into light and love, returning to the source of creation.

Gratitude and Closing:

Express gratitude to your ancestors for their presence, guidance, and the opportunity to heal your ancestral lineage.
Blow out the candle, symbolizing the completion of the spell and the dispersal of healing energy into the universe.

Note: This spell is a personal and introspective practice. Feel free to adapt the instructions, incantation, and ritual elements according to your own beliefs and ancestral connections. Approach the spell with reverence, respect, and an open heart, allowing the healing energies to flow through your ancestral lineage. Remember that healing ancestral wounds is a process that may require ongoing work and self-reflection.

Spell for Breaking Financial Barriers

Tools:

Green candle
A small bowl of salt or rice
A piece of citrine or pyrite crystal
Pen and paper
A lighter or matches
Instructions:

Preparation:

Find a quiet and undisturbed space where you can perform the spell.
Set up your altar or sacred space with the green candle, bowl of salt or rice, citrine or pyrite crystal, pen and paper, and the lighter or matches.

Clearing and Grounding:

Take a few deep breaths to center yourself and clear your mind.
Light the green candle, representing financial abundance and prosperity.
Hold the crystal in your hands and visualize grounding energy flowing through you, connecting you to the Earth's abundance.

Setting Intentions:

Write down your financial goals and intentions on the piece of paper. Be specific about what you desire to manifest and the financial barriers you want to break.
Hold the paper between your hands and infuse it with your intentions and energy. Focus on your goals and imagine yourself overcoming financial obstacles with ease and grace.

Charging the Crystal:

Place the crystal on top of the paper, allowing its energy to absorb your intentions. Visualize the crystal radiating golden light, amplifying your intentions and attracting financial abundance.

Incantation:

Recite the following incantation or create your own, speaking with conviction and belief in your financial empowerment:

> "By the power of my will and the energy of this crystal,
> I break through financial barriers, dispelling lack and dismissal.
> Abundance flows to me, in all forms and ways,
> I release all limitations and claim my prosperous days."

Symbolic Action:

Take a pinch of salt or rice from the bowl and sprinkle it over the crystal and paper, symbolizing the clearing of financial blockages and the activation of abundance.

Candle Ritual:

Hold your hands over the candle, feeling the warmth and energy of the flame.
Visualize the flame as a transformative force that dissolves financial barriers and opens doors to prosperity.
Pass the paper and crystal through the flame, allowing the fire to cleanse and energize them.

Gratitude and Release:

Express gratitude to the universe and the divine for the abundance that is coming your way.
Blow out the candle, symbolizing the completion of the spell and the release of your intentions into the universe.

Action Steps:

After performing the spell, take inspired action towards your financial goals.
Remain open to opportunities, be proactive, and make wise financial decisions.

Note: This spell is a tool for manifestation and breaking through financial barriers. It is important to combine it with practical action, responsible financial management, and a positive mindset. Trust in the process and believe in your ability to create abundance in your life.

Spell for Enhancing Connection with Elemental Forces

Tools:

Four colored candles representing the elements: red for fire, blue for water, green for earth, and yellow for air.
A small dish of salt or soil to represent earth.
A small bowl of water.
A feather or incense stick to represent air.
A lighter or matches.
Optional: crystals or gemstones associated with the elements (e.g., ruby for fire, aquamarine for water, moss agate for earth, citrine for air).
Instructions:

Preparation:

Find a quiet and comfortable space where you can perform the spell.
Set up your altar or sacred space with the four colored candles, the dish of salt or soil, the bowl of water, the feather or incense stick, and any optional crystals or gemstones.

Centering and Grounding:

Take a few deep breaths to center yourself and clear your mind.
Light the candles in the order of fire, water, earth, and air, moving clockwise around your altar.
Focus on each element as you light its corresponding candle, connecting with its energy and presence.

Invocation:

Stand in the center of your sacred space and face each direction, starting with the east (representing air), then moving to the south (fire), west (water), and north (earth).
As you face each direction, recite an invocation or prayer to invoke the power and presence of the elemental force, using your own words or the following example:

> "Oh, element of [name the element],
> I call upon your primal essence,
> Grant me connection and deep understanding,
> Align my energy with your divine presence."

Repeat the invocation for each direction, visualizing the element's energy enveloping you and establishing a strong connection.

Elemental Offerings:

As a sign of respect and gratitude, place a small offering associated with each element on your altar or in the respective directions:
Fire: Offer a small piece of charcoal or a dried chili pepper.
Water: Offer a few drops of natural essential oil or a seashell.
Earth: Offer a pinch of herbs or a small stone.
Air: Wave the feather or incense stick over the altar, allowing its smoke to waft through the air.

Elemental Meditation:

Sit or stand in front of your altar, facing the center.
Close your eyes and imagine each element surrounding you, one at a time.
Envision the qualities and energies of each element merging with your own, creating a harmonious connection.
Spend a few moments with each element, feeling its presence and absorbing its wisdom and power.

Gratitude and Release:

Express gratitude to the elemental forces for their presence and guidance.
Blow out the candles one by one, starting with air, then earth, water, and finally fire, moving counterclockwise around your altar.
Feel a sense of completion and release, knowing that the elemental energies will continue to support and guide you.

Note: This spell is intended to deepen your connection with the elemental forces and enhance your understanding of their energies. Always approach working with elemental forces with respect and reverence. Customize the spell and offerings based on your own intuition and relationship with the elements.

Spell for Banishing Negative Influences from Dreams

Tools:

White candle
Pen and paper
Small fireproof dish or bowl
Matches or lighter

Instructions:

Preparation:

Find a quiet and comfortable space where you can perform the spell without interruptions.
Set up your sacred space by placing the white candle on a clean and safe surface.
Have the pen and paper, as well as the fireproof dish or bowl, nearby.

Centering and Focus:

Take a few deep breaths to calm your mind and center yourself.
Light the white candle, symbolizing purity and protection.
Sit or stand in front of the candle and focus your attention on its flame, letting it draw your focus inward.

Clearing Intention:

Take the pen and paper and write down a clear and specific intention to banish negative influences from your dreams.
Use your own words or try the following example: "I release and banish all negative energies and influences from my dreams. I invite only positive and uplifting experiences while I sleep. May my dreams be filled with peace, insight, and healing."

Burning Ritual:

Hold the paper with your written intention over the candle flame, allowing it to catch fire.
Safely place the burning paper into the fireproof dish or bowl, watching it burn completely.

As the paper burns, visualize all negative influences and energies being consumed by the flames, transforming into pure energy and dissipating.

Affirmation and Protection:

Repeat the following affirmation out loud or silently: "I am protected and surrounded by positive energies. My dreams are safe and free from negativity. I awaken refreshed and empowered."

Closing:

Allow the candle to burn out on its own or extinguish it safely.
Take a moment to reflect on the spell and the intention you have set, feeling a sense of peace and release.
Dispose of the ashes from the burnt paper in a respectful manner, such as burying them in the earth or scattering them in flowing water.

Note: This spell is intended to help banish negative influences from your dreams and promote more positive and uplifting dream experiences. It's essential to approach the spell with a clear intention and a belief in its effectiveness. You may repeat this spell as often as needed or adapt it to suit your personal preferences. Always prioritize your safety when working with candles and fire.

Spell for Restoring Balance and Harmony

Tools:

White candle
Small dish or bowl
Clear quartz crystal
Pen and paper

Instructions:

Preparation:

Find a quiet and peaceful space where you can perform the spell without distractions.
Set up your sacred space by placing the white candle in the center and the dish or bowl nearby.
Hold the clear quartz crystal in your hands and take a few moments to ground yourself.
Invocation of Balance:

Light the white candle, symbolizing purity and balance.
Close your eyes and take a deep breath, focusing on restoring harmony and balance in your life.

Say the following incantation, or create your own words:

> "By the light of this candle's flame,
> I call upon balance, I call upon the same.
> Restore harmony, restore equilibrium,
> Let peace and serenity fill every room."

Writing Intentions:

Take the pen and paper and write down specific areas of your life where you seek balance and harmony.
Reflect on aspects such as relationships, work, health, emotions, and spirituality.
Phrase your intentions positively, focusing on what you desire to bring into balance rather than what you want to eliminate.

Crystal Charging:

Hold the clear quartz crystal in your hands and visualize it being filled with radiant, balancing energy.
Envision the crystal absorbing any imbalances or disharmonies within you or your surroundings.
Place the crystal in the dish or bowl next to the candle.

Affirmation and Release:

Read your written intentions aloud, affirming your commitment to restoring balance and harmony.
Lightly touch the crystal with your fingertips, infusing it with your intentions and energy.
Visualize the crystal radiating a bright, harmonizing light, dispersing balance and harmony throughout your being and environment.

Closing:

Express gratitude for the balance and harmony that you have invoked.
Allow the candle to burn down completely or extinguish it safely.
Keep the crystal in a sacred space or carry it with you as a reminder of your intention to maintain balance and harmony.

Note: This spell is intended to help restore balance and harmony in various areas of your life. It's essential to approach the spell with sincerity, clarity of intention, and a belief in its effectiveness. Feel free to customize the spell to align with your personal preferences and needs. Always prioritize safety when working with candles and fire.

Spell for Strengthening Spiritual Communication

Tools:

Purple candle
Amethyst crystal
Incense (such as frankincense or sandalwood)
Pen and paper

Instructions:

Preparation:

Find a quiet and sacred space where you can perform the spell without interruptions.
Set up your altar by placing the purple candle in the center and the amethyst crystal and incense nearby.
Take a few moments to ground yourself and clear your mind.

Invocation of Spiritual Communication:

Light the purple candle, symbolizing spiritual connection and insight.
Light the incense, allowing its fragrance to fill the space and create an atmosphere of sacredness.
Close your eyes and take a deep breath, focusing on opening yourself to enhanced spiritual communication.

Say the following incantation, or create your own words:

> "With this flame, I ignite the channel,
> Open the pathways for spiritual knowledge to travel.
> Strengthen my intuition, sharpen my sight,
> Guide me in communing with realms of light."

Crystal Activation:

Hold the amethyst crystal in your hands and visualize it being infused with vibrant and pure energy.
Envision the crystal amplifying your spiritual senses and facilitating clear and meaningful communication with the spiritual realms.

Place the crystal in a prominent position near the candle.

Writing Intentions:

Take the pen and paper and write down your intentions for strengthening spiritual communication.
Be specific about the type of communication you wish to enhance, such as connecting with spirit guides, receiving intuitive guidance, or deepening your connection with higher realms.
Phrase your intentions positively, focusing on the clarity, depth, and authenticity of the communication.

Affirmation and Visualization:

Read your written intentions aloud, infusing them with your energy and intention.
Lightly touch the amethyst crystal with your fingertips, visualizing it radiating a powerful and purifying light.
See yourself surrounded by a sphere of divine energy that supports and enhances your spiritual communication.

Closing:

Express gratitude for the strengthened spiritual communication that you have invoked.
Allow the candle to burn down completely or extinguish it safely.
Keep the amethyst crystal in a sacred space or carry it with you as a reminder of your intention to deepen your spiritual communication.

Note: This spell is designed to enhance your ability to connect and communicate with the spiritual realms. Approach the spell with reverence, clarity of intention, and a belief in the power of spiritual communication. Feel free to adapt the spell to align with your personal preferences and needs. Remember to exercise caution when working with candles and fire.

Spell for Attracting Positive Energy

Tools:

Yellow or white candle
Clear quartz crystal
Essential oil (such as lavender, lemon, or rosemary)
Pen and paper

Instructions:

Preparation:

Find a peaceful and quiet space where you can perform the spell without distractions.
Set up your altar by placing the yellow or white candle in the center and the clear quartz crystal nearby.
Take a moment to center yourself and clear your mind.

Candle Blessing:

Light the yellow or white candle, symbolizing the infusion of positive energy into your space.
Hold your hands over the flame, allowing the warmth to radiate through your palms.

Say the following incantation, or create your own words:

> "Candle of light, I call upon your glow,
> To attract positive energy, let it flow.
> With every flicker, negativity is released,
> Inviting abundance and blessings increased."

Crystal Activation:

Take the clear quartz crystal in your hands and focus on its energy.
Visualize the crystal becoming charged with powerful positive vibrations.
Place the crystal next to the candle, allowing it to amplify and radiate positive energy throughout the space.
Aromatherapy:

Add a few drops of your chosen essential oil to a diffuser or oil burner.
As the scent fills the air, take a deep breath and inhale the uplifting aroma.

Visualize the fragrance purifying and revitalizing the energy in your surroundings, attracting positive energies.

Writing Affirmations:

Take the pen and paper and write down positive affirmations that reflect the energy you wish to attract.
Use empowering and affirmative language to state your intentions clearly and positively. For example, "I am a magnet for positive opportunities and abundance," or "I attract joy, love, and harmony into my life."

Affirmation and Visualization:

Read your written affirmations aloud with conviction and belief.
Close your eyes and visualize yourself surrounded by a vibrant aura of positive energy. See this energy drawing positive experiences, people, and circumstances into your life.

Gratitude and Closing:

Express gratitude for the positive energy that you have invoked and the blessings it will bring.
Allow the candle to burn down completely or extinguish it safely.
Keep the clear quartz crystal in a prominent place, such as your altar or a sacred space, as a reminder of the positive energy you are attracting.

Note: Remember that attracting positive energy starts from within. Approach this spell with an open heart, a positive mindset, and a willingness to embrace the changes and opportunities that come your way. Adapt the spell to suit your personal preferences and needs. Exercise caution when working with candles and fire.

Spell for Unlocking Inner Wisdom

Tools:

Purple candle
Amethyst crystal
Pen and paper
Divination tool of choice (such as tarot cards, oracle cards, or a pendulum)

Instructions:

Preparation:

Find a quiet and comfortable space where you can focus without interruptions.
Create your sacred space by setting up your altar. Place the purple candle in the center and the amethyst crystal nearby.
Take a few moments to ground yourself and clear your mind through deep breathing and centering.

Candle Blessing:

Light the purple candle, symbolizing the connection to your higher wisdom and inner guidance.
As the flame flickers, visualize it illuminating the path to your inner wisdom and opening the channels of intuitive knowledge.

Say the following incantation, or create your own words:

> "Candle of purple light, guide me on this quest,
> Unlock the wisdom within, let my soul be blessed.
> From deep within my being, let knowledge freely flow,
> Illuminate my path, the answers I shall know."

Crystal Connection:

Hold the amethyst crystal in your hands and take a moment to connect with its energy.
Feel the calming and supportive vibrations of the crystal.
Envision the amethyst amplifying your intuitive abilities and enhancing your connection to your inner wisdom.

Invocation:

With the pen and paper, write down a question or topic for which you seek guidance or insight.
Place your hands on either side of the paper, forming a connection between your energy and the question.
Focus your intention on unlocking your inner wisdom and gaining clarity.

Divination:

Choose your preferred divination tool (tarot cards, oracle cards, or pendulum).
Hold the tool in your hands and ask for guidance and insights regarding your question or topic.
Shuffle the cards or hold the pendulum and allow your intuition to guide you in selecting the cards or receiving answers through the pendulum's movements.
Pay close attention to the messages and symbols presented to you, trusting your intuition to interpret their meanings.

Reflection and Meditation:

Take a moment to reflect on the messages received and the insights gained.
Lightly close your eyes and enter into a meditative state.
Visualize a stream of purple light flowing from the candle and the amethyst crystal into your mind and heart, filling you with clarity, wisdom, and insight.
Allow any additional thoughts or revelations to come to you during this meditative state.

Closing:

Express gratitude for the wisdom and guidance received during this practice.
Allow the candle to burn down completely or extinguish it safely.
Keep the amethyst crystal in a sacred space or carry it with you to enhance your connection to your inner wisdom.

Note: Trust your intuition and inner guidance throughout this spell. Adapt the spell to suit your personal preferences and needs. Remember that inner wisdom often unfolds over time, so be open to receiving insights beyond the immediate practice. Exercise caution when working with candles and fire.

Spell for Healing Past-Life Traumas

Tools:

White candle
Selenite crystal
Pen and paper
Healing incense (such as lavender or frankincense)

Instructions:

Preparation:

Find a quiet and comfortable space where you can focus without interruptions.
Create your sacred space by setting up your altar. Place the white candle in the center and the selenite crystal nearby.
Light the healing incense to purify the space and create a calming atmosphere.

Candle Blessing:

Light the white candle, symbolizing purity and healing energy.
As the flame dances, visualize it cleansing and purifying your energetic field, releasing any past-life traumas or imprints.

Say the following incantation, or create your own words:

> "Candle of white light, I call upon your healing power,
> Release the wounds of the past, restore balance and flower.
> From ancient times to now, let the scars be mended,
> Healing the traumas, in this life and those extended."

Crystal Connection:

Hold the selenite crystal in your hands and feel its calming and purifying energy.
Envision the crystal as a conduit for divine healing light, penetrating deep into your being and gently releasing past-life traumas.
Set the intention that the selenite assists in healing and clearing any residual energy that no longer serves you.

Invocation:

With the pen and paper, write down any recurring patterns, fears, or challenges in your life that you suspect might be connected to past-life traumas.
Take a moment to connect with your higher self and ask for guidance and healing in addressing these traumas.
Offer a prayer or affirmation, expressing your intention to release and heal past-life wounds for your highest good.

Visualization and Affirmation:

Close your eyes and enter into a relaxed state.
Visualize a healing light surrounding you, gradually expanding to envelop your entire being.
See this light penetrating deeply into your cells, dissolving and transmuting any negative imprints or traumas.

Repeat the following affirmation, or create your own words:

> "I release the past, its wounds no longer bind,
> Healing light fills every space, true freedom I find.
> Past-life traumas dissolve, their power no more,
> I am healed, whole, and at peace to my core."

Energy Healing:

Hold the selenite crystal in your dominant hand and gently pass it over your body, starting from your head and moving down to your feet.
Imagine the crystal drawing out any stagnant or negative energies associated with past-life traumas.
Allow yourself to feel the healing and soothing energy flowing through you, bringing balance and release.

Gratitude and Closure:

Express gratitude to the divine, your higher self, and any spiritual guides or beings who supported you in this healing process.
Snuff out the candle or allow it to burn down completely.
Keep the selenite crystal in a sacred space or carry it with you as a reminder of your healing journey.

Note: This spell is intended to assist in the healing of past-life traumas. It is essential to approach this practice with self-care, self-compassion, and an open heart. Remember that healing is a process, and it may take time for complete resolution. Trust your intuition and adjust the spell as needed to suit your personal beliefs and preferences.

Spell for Protection During Ritual Work

Tools:

Black candle
Amethyst crystal
Frankincense or sandalwood incense
Pen and paper
Salt or protective herbs (such as sage or rosemary)

Instructions:

Preparation:

Find a quiet and sacred space where you will conduct your ritual work.
Set up your altar or workspace, placing the black candle in the center and the amethyst crystal nearby.
Light the frankincense or sandalwood incense to purify the space and create a protective atmosphere.

Candle Blessing:

Light the black candle, symbolizing protection and grounding energy.
Focus on the flame and visualize it forming a shield of darkness around you, warding off any negative or harmful energies.

Say the following incantation, or create your own words:

> "Candle of black, guardian of the night,
> Protect and shield me with your might.
> As I work my magic, keep me safe and secure,
> Ward off all harm, of that I am sure."

Crystal Empowerment:

Hold the amethyst crystal in your hands and connect with its protective and spiritual properties.
Envision the crystal radiating a soothing purple light, forming a shield of energy around you.
Set the intention that the amethyst acts as a conduit for divine protection, enhancing your intuitive and psychic abilities.

Protective Symbols:

Take the pen and paper and draw any protective symbols or sigils that resonate with you.
Visualize these symbols as a potent shield of protection, surrounding you and your ritual space.
Place the paper with the symbols on your altar or keep it close during your ritual work.
Salt or Herb Circle:

Sprinkle a circle of salt or protective herbs around your workspace, symbolizing a boundary of protection.
Envision this circle as an impenetrable barrier that repels any negative or unwanted energies.
As you create the circle, say the following incantation, or create your own words:

> "By salt (or herbs) I cast this circle round,
> Protection strong, no negativity found.
> Within this space, I am safe and secure,
> No harm shall enter, of that I am sure."

Invocation of Protection:

Close your eyes and center yourself, connecting with your higher self and any deities or spiritual guides you work with.
Invoke their presence and ask for their protection during your ritual work.

Say the following incantation, or create your own words:

> "I call upon the guardians of light,
> Protect me with your power, strong and bright.
> Shield me from harm, both seen and unseen,
> As I walk this path, keep my energy clean."

Energy Cleansing:

Stand or sit in the center of your protected space and take a few deep breaths.
Visualize a beam of pure white light descending from above, flowing through your entire being.
Feel this light purifying and cleansing your energy, removing any negativity or interference.
Allow the light to fill you with a sense of strength, clarity, and protection.

Gratitude and Closure:

Express gratitude to the divine, your higher self, and any spiritual guides or beings who have protected you.
Extinguish the black candle or allow it to burn down completely.
Dispose of the salt or protective herbs, returning them to the Earth with gratitude.

Note: This spell is designed to create a protective energy field during ritual work. Adapt the spell as needed to align with your personal beliefs and preferences. Trust your intuition and modify any aspects of the spell to suit your specific needs. Remember to approach ritual work with respect, mindfulness, and responsible intention.

Spell for Strengthening Psychic Shields

Tools:

Black candle
Amethyst crystal
Frankincense or sandalwood incense
Pen and paper
A small dish of salt or protective herbs (such as rosemary or basil)

Instructions:

Preparation:

Find a quiet and undisturbed space where you can focus on strengthening your psychic shields.
Set up your altar or workspace, placing the black candle in the center and the amethyst crystal nearby.
Light the frankincense or sandalwood incense to create a protective and sacred atmosphere.

Candle Blessing:

Light the black candle, symbolizing protection and the absorption of negative energy. Gaze into the flame and visualize it as a powerful shield, guarding you against any psychic intrusion or harm.

Say the following incantation, or create your own words:

> "Candle of black, shield of might,
> Protect me well through day and night.
> As I fortify my psychic wall,
> Ward off all that may enthrall."

Crystal Empowerment:

Hold the amethyst crystal in your hands and connect with its protective and intuitive properties.
Envision the crystal as a shield of light, surrounding you with a powerful and impenetrable barrier against negative influences.

Set the intention that the crystal enhances your psychic shields, filters out negativity, and promotes clarity and insight.

Intention Setting:

Take the pen and paper and write down your intentions for strengthening your psychic shields.
Be specific and focus on the qualities or aspects you wish to enhance, such as psychic protection, intuitive discernment, or energy boundary setting.
Once you have written your intentions, hold the paper between your hands and infuse it with your energy and intent.

Salt or Herb Blessing:

Place the small dish of salt or protective herbs in front of the candle.
Sprinkle a pinch of salt or herbs onto the paper with your intentions, symbolizing the fortification of your psychic shields.

Say the following incantation, or create your own words:

> "By earth and salt (or herbs) this spell is bound,
> Strengthening my shields, all negative energies confound.
> Protect my mind, my spirit, and my soul,
> Let only positive energies take control."

Invocation of Psychic Guidance:

Close your eyes and take a few moments to center yourself.
Call upon your spirit guides, guardian angels, or any psychic beings you work with, inviting their guidance and support in strengthening your psychic shields.

Say the following incantation, or create your own words:

> "Guides and guardians of the psychic plane,
> Aid me in my quest, protect me from all strain.
> Strengthen my shields, so pure and strong,
> Shield me from harm, all the day long."

Meditation and Visualization:

Sit comfortably in front of the candle and crystal.
Close your eyes and enter a meditative state.

Visualize yourself surrounded by a brilliant purple or white light, representing your fortified psychic shields.
See this light extending outward, forming an impenetrable shield around you, blocking any negative or intrusive energies.
Feel the sense of safety, peace, and empowerment that comes with your strengthened psychic shields.

Gratitude and Closure:

Express gratitude to the divine, your guides, and any beings of light who have assisted you.
Extinguish the black candle, or allow it to burn down completely if it is safe to do so.
Keep the amethyst crystal on your altar or carry it with you as a reminder of your empowered psychic shields.

Remember that this spell serves as a tool to strengthen your own inherent psychic abilities and intuition. Regular practice, self-reflection, and continued learning are essential for nurturing and maintaining your psychic shields.

Spell for Manifesting Spiritual Growth

Tools:

Purple candle
Clear quartz crystal
Patchouli or lavender incense
Pen and paper
A small dish of salt or grounding herbs (such as sage or cedar)

Instructions:

Preparation:

Find a quiet and sacred space where you can focus on your spiritual growth.
Set up your altar or workspace, placing the purple candle in the center and the clear quartz crystal nearby.
Light the patchouli or lavender incense to create a serene and spiritual atmosphere.

Candle Blessing:

Light the purple candle, symbolizing spiritual growth, transformation, and connection to higher realms.
Focus on the flame and visualize it as a beacon of divine light, guiding you on your path of spiritual development.

Say the following incantation, or create your own words:

> "Candle of purple, flame so bright,
> Illuminate my path, bring spiritual light.
> As I seek growth and wisdom deep,
> Manifest my desires, my soul to keep."

Crystal Empowerment:

Hold the clear quartz crystal in your hands and connect with its amplifying and clarifying properties.
Envision the crystal as a conduit for spiritual energy, radiating a pure and uplifting vibration.
Set the intention that the crystal enhances your spiritual growth, clears blockages, and attunes you to higher wisdom.

Intention Setting:

Take the pen and paper and write down your intentions for spiritual growth and development.
Be specific and focus on the qualities or areas you wish to enhance, such as intuition, wisdom, or connection to spirit.
Once you have written your intentions, hold the paper between your hands and infuse it with your energy and intent.

Salt or Herb Blessing:

Place the small dish of salt or grounding herbs in front of the candle.
Sprinkle a pinch of salt or herbs onto the paper with your intentions, symbolizing the grounding and anchoring of your spiritual growth.

Say the following incantation, or create your own words:

> "By earth and salt (or herbs) this spell is bound,
> Grounding my growth, with strength I am crowned.
> As I align with higher realms and divine,
> My spirit expands, with clarity I shine."

Invocation of Guidance:

Close your eyes and take a few moments to center yourself.
Call upon your spiritual guides, guardian angels, or deities you work with, inviting their guidance and support in your spiritual journey.

Say the following incantation, or create your own words:

> "Guides and guardians, hear my call,
> Assist me in my spiritual rise, both large and small.
> Show me the way, reveal what's true,
> Deepen my connection, as I journey anew."

Meditation and Visualization:

Sit comfortably in front of the candle and crystal.
Close your eyes and enter a meditative state.
Visualize yourself surrounded by a radiant purple light, symbolizing spiritual energy and growth.

See yourself embracing new knowledge, wisdom, and experiences that expand your spiritual awareness.
Feel the joy, fulfillment, and empowerment that come with your spiritual growth.
Gratitude and Closure:

Express gratitude to the divine, your guides, and any beings of light who have supported you.
Extinguish the purple candle, or allow it to burn down completely if it is safe to do so.
Keep the clear quartz crystal on your altar or carry it with you as a reminder of your intention for spiritual growth.

Note: This spell is meant to support and enhance your spiritual journey. Remember that true growth comes from within and through consistent practice and dedication. Be open to the signs, lessons, and opportunities that come your way as you walk the path of spiritual growth.

CHAPTER 4
Unveiling the Shadows

Disclaimer:
The following section explores the darker aspects of ancient Babylonian religion. It is crucial to approach these practices with caution, respect, and a deep understanding of their historical and cultural context. They should not be taken lightly or used for harmful purposes. The intention is to provide a comprehensive understanding of the beliefs and practices of ancient Babylonian religion, but it is strongly advised against attempting to perform these rituals or incantations in the present day. Instead, it is recommended to focus on the historical and cultural understanding of these practices to gain insights into the ancient Babylonian civilization.

Exploring Ancient Babylon's Rituals

Welcome to the intriguing journey into the lesser-known aspects of ancient Babylonian religion. In this chapter, we will delve into the darker side of their belief system, shedding light on practices that were both mysterious and potent. It is important to approach this exploration with caution and respect, as we navigate the shadows of an ancient civilization.

Ancient Babylonian religion was a complex tapestry of beliefs and rituals, encompassing both light and dark elements. While much of our understanding has focused on the positive and benevolent aspects, it is equally important to acknowledge the presence of practices that delved into the realm of the occult, sorcery, and darker forces. This chapter aims to provide insight into these practices while emphasizing the significance of historical and cultural context.

However, it is crucial to note that these practices should not be taken lightly or used for harmful purposes. Our primary goal is to foster a comprehensive understanding of ancient Babylonian religion and its various facets. By examining the darker aspects, we can gain a more complete picture of the beliefs and rituals that shaped this ancient civilization.

We must remember that we are observers, students of history, and not practitioners. It is strongly advised against attempting to perform the rituals or incantations described in this chapter in the present day. Instead, our focus should be on acquiring knowledge and deepening our appreciation for the rich cultural heritage of ancient Babylon.

Through this exploration, we aim to shed light on the shadows and expand our understanding of ancient Babylonian religion. By embracing a respectful and informed approach, we can navigate this intriguing realm and gain insights into the complexities of their spiritual practices.

So, let us embark on this enlightening journey into the dark side of ancient Babylonian religion, guided by curiosity, respect, and a commitment to cultural understanding.

Dark Deities and Demonic Entities

The existence of deities and entities associated with darker aspects in Babylonian mythology.

In this chapter, we will embark on a fascinating exploration of the existence of deities and entities associated with the darker aspects of Babylonian mythology. While the Babylonian pantheon is often associated with benevolent gods and goddesses, there exists a realm of shadow and mystery that encompasses a host of intriguing beings. We will delve into their origins, characteristics, and roles within the Babylonian cosmology, shedding light on their significance and the narratives that surround them.

The Underworld Deities:

Within Babylonian mythology, the concept of the underworld held profound significance in shaping the cosmological beliefs of the ancient Babylonians. It was believed to be a realm that existed beneath the surface of the Earth, serving as the abode of the deceased and the dwelling place of deities and entities associated with darkness, decay, and the mysteries of the afterlife. This realm was governed by a powerful goddess known as Ereshkigal, who held unparalleled authority and power over the deceased.

Ereshkigal, the goddess of the underworld, played a pivotal role in the Babylonian pantheon. She was revered as the ruler of the land of the dead, presiding over the spirits and souls who journeyed to the underworld after their mortal existence ended. Ereshkigal's domain was a realm of shadows and silence, where the souls of the departed faced judgment and underwent various trials and transformations.

The authority of Ereshkigal cannot be underestimated, as she was considered an essential figure in maintaining the balance between the realms of the living and the dead. She held the power to grant or deny entry to souls, ensuring the proper order and harmony in the afterlife. Ereshkigal was both feared and respected, embodying the enigmatic nature of death and the profound mysteries that awaited beyond the threshold of mortality.

In studying Ereshkigal and her counterparts, such as Nergal, the god of war and plague associated with the underworld, we gain invaluable insights into the ancient Babylonian's perception of life, death, and the spiritual realm. These deities, along with the rituals and beliefs surrounding them, provided a framework for understanding the cyclical nature of existence and the complex relationship between the mortal realm and the afterlife.

The Babylonians believed that their actions in life would have consequences in the afterlife, and therefore, the veneration of underworld deities played a crucial role in their religious practices. Rituals and offerings were made to appease and honor these deities, seeking their protection and guidance in navigating the mysteries of the afterlife. Through the study of Ereshkigal and her role as the goddess of the underworld, we can grasp the profound influence that the realm of the dead had on the ancient Babylonian culture and their spiritual beliefs.

By delving into the intricate relationship between life, death, and the spiritual realm in ancient Babylonian culture, we deepen our understanding of their cosmological framework. The mythology surrounding Ereshkigal and her counterparts offers profound insights into the ancient Babylonian's views on mortality, the journey of the soul, and the interconnectedness of the spiritual and earthly realms. It highlights the profound significance they placed on honoring the deceased and the complexities inherent in their perception of the afterlife.

Example:
Consider the mythological narrative of Inanna's descent into the underworld, where she confronts Ereshkigal. This tale highlights the intricate balance between the forces of light and darkness, as well as the transformative power of the underworld and the trials one must face to attain enlightenment.

In the biblical context, there is a story that shares some thematic similarities with Inanna's descent into the underworld. It is the story of Jesus' crucifixion, death, and resurrection. Although the details and characters differ, both narratives explore the themes of descent, confrontation with darkness, and the transformative journey towards enlightenment.

In the New Testament of the Bible, the Gospels recount the events leading up to Jesus' crucifixion and subsequent resurrection. Jesus, who is believed to be the Son of God, willingly undergoes the ordeal of crucifixion, descending into darkness and death. This sacrificial act is seen as a confrontation with the forces of darkness and evil, representing the ultimate struggle between good and evil.

Similar to Inanna's descent into the underworld, Jesus' journey through death symbolizes a transformative process. It is through his death and resurrection that he overcomes darkness and offers the promise of salvation and enlightenment to his followers. The story emphasizes the concept of spiritual rebirth and the triumph of light over darkness.

While the specific details of the narratives differ, both Inanna's descent into the underworld and Jesus' crucifixion and resurrection explore the themes of confronting darkness, undergoing trials, and attaining enlightenment or salvation. They symbolize the universal human journey of facing challenges, overcoming obstacles, and finding redemption or spiritual growth.

It is important to note that while these narratives share similar themes, they belong to different cultural and religious contexts. The Babylonian myth of Inanna's descent into the underworld predates the biblical story of Jesus' crucifixion and resurrection. Therefore, any connections or similarities between the two should be understood within their respective cultural and historical contexts.

Problem:
Reflect upon the significance of the underworld deities in Babylonian mythology and discuss their role in shaping the beliefs and practices of the ancient Babylonians.

Exercise:
Create a comparative analysis between the underworld deities in Babylonian mythology and their counterparts in other ancient mythologies, such as the Greek Hades and the Egyptian Osiris.

Malevolent Spirits and Demonic Entities

Within the rich tapestry of Babylonian mythology, the existence of malevolent spirits and demonic entities occupies a prominent place, representing the darker aspects of the spiritual realm. These entities, known as utukku and lilû, were believed to wield significant power and influence over human lives, capable of causing illness, nightmares, and misfortune. Exploring their origins and characteristics offers valuable insights into the Babylonian perception of evil and the methods they employed to safeguard themselves against these malevolent forces.

In Babylonian belief, the utukku were spirits associated with disease and calamity. They were thought to be the restless souls of the deceased who had not found peace in the afterlife. These spirits were often considered to be the result of unfinished business or unresolved conflicts during their earthly existence. They were believed to roam the mortal realm, seeking to bring affliction and suffering upon the living.

The lilû, on the other hand, were demonic entities associated with night terrors and sexual desires. They were often depicted as nocturnal creatures, lurking in the darkness and preying upon unsuspecting individuals. These malevolent beings were believed to be powerful and capable of inflicting harm on both the physical and psychological well-being of their victims.

To protect themselves from these malevolent forces, the Babylonians developed various rituals, incantations, and amulets. They sought to establish a barrier between the mortal world and the realms of darkness, invoking the aid of benevolent deities and employing magical practices. Rituals of purification, invocations of protective deities, and the use of amulets adorned with symbols of divine power were common methods used to ward off these malevolent spirits.

Understanding the Babylonian perception of evil and their strategies for protection provides a glimpse into their worldview and the challenges they faced in navigating the spiritual realm. It reveals their belief in the existence of unseen forces that could bring harm and disruption to their lives, and their fervent efforts to safeguard themselves from such influences. Exploring the mythology surrounding utukku and lilû deepens our understanding of ancient Babylonian culture and their complex relationship with the supernatural world.

Example:
The Enuma Elish, the Babylonian creation myth, portrays the struggle between the primordial forces of chaos and order. In this epic tale, Tiamat, a powerful and destructive deity, embodies the chaotic and dark aspects of the universe, while Marduk, the patron god of Babylon, emerges as the triumphant force of order and light.

Problem:
Examine the ways in which the Babylonians sought protection from malevolent spirits and demonic entities and discuss the significance of these practices in their society.

Exercise:
Research and analyze different protective rituals or incantations used by the ancient Babylonians to ward off malevolent spirits, and create your own ritual based on their principles.

Conclusion:
Exploring the existence of deities and entities associated with the darker aspects in Babylonian mythology provides valuable insights into the complex worldview of the ancient Babylonians. By examining the underworld deities, malevolent spirits, and demonic entities, we gain a comprehensive understanding of the intricate balance between light and darkness in their religious beliefs. As students of new-age studies, it is essential to approach these topics with respect, curiosity, and a desire to deepen our knowledge of ancient Babylonian mythology and its spiritual landscape.

Descriptions and stories related to deities such as Nergal (god of war and pestilence) and Ereshkigal (goddess of the underworld).

Deities in ancient Babylonian mythology played diverse and significant roles, representing various aspects of life and the natural world. Two notable deities are Nergal, the god of war and pestilence, and Ereshkigal, the goddess of the underworld. Exploring their characteristics, myths, and cultural significance offers invaluable insights into the Babylonian pantheon and their religious beliefs.

Nergal, often depicted as a fearsome warrior, was associated with both destructive and regenerative forces. As the god of war, he personified the relentless power and violence of battle. Babylonian mythology tells stories of Nergal's exploits in battle, showcasing his strength and ferocity. However, Nergal was not solely focused on war. He also represented the transformative aspects of destruction and pestilence, which were seen as necessary for renewal and rebirth. In this context, Nergal's association with disease and pestilence was believed to bring about purging and cleansing, clearing the path for new growth and revitalization.

Ereshkigal, the goddess of the underworld, held a prominent place in Babylonian mythology. She governed the realm of the dead, where the souls of the deceased journeyed after their earthly lives ended. Ereshkigal was often depicted as a powerful and formidable figure, embodying the mysteries of death and the afterlife. One of the most famous myths involving Ereshkigal is the story of Inanna's descent into the underworld. This narrative portrays Ereshkigal as a formidable guardian of the realm, subjecting Inanna to a series of trials and challenges. Through this myth, the Babylonians explored the concepts of mortality, transformation, and the cyclical nature of life.

Studying the characteristics and stories of deities like Nergal and Ereshkigal allows us to delve into the complex belief system of ancient Babylonian culture. It enables us to understand the significance of war and pestilence as both destructive and transformative forces in their worldview. Furthermore, exploring the mythology surrounding Ereshkigal provides insights into their understanding of death, the afterlife, and the role of the underworld in the cycle of existence.

To deepen your understanding of these deities, consider engaging in the following exercises:

Research and analyze additional myths and stories related to Nergal and Ereshkigal, noting the different aspects of their personalities and the lessons conveyed through their narratives.

Compare the characteristics and roles of Nergal and Ereshkigal with deities from other mythological systems, such as the war gods of Greek mythology or the underworld deities in Egyptian mythology. Discuss the similarities and differences in their representations and cultural significance.

Reflect on the symbolic meanings associated with war, pestilence, and the underworld in ancient Babylonian society. How might these concepts have influenced their perspectives on life, death, and the human condition?

Imagine you are an ancient Babylonian priest or priestess. Write a prayer or invocation to either Nergal or Ereshkigal, expressing your understanding of their powers and seeking their guidance or protection in a specific aspect of life.

By engaging in these exercises, you will develop a deeper appreciation for the complexities of ancient Babylonian mythology and gain insights into the cultural, religious, and philosophical dimensions of Nergal and Ereshkigal.

Roles in ancient Babylonian religion and the rituals and incantations dedicated to them.

Nergal and Ereshkigal, prominent deities in ancient Babylonian mythology, held significant roles within the religious practices of the time. The Babylonians recognized their power and influence, dedicating rituals and incantations to these revered figures. By exploring their roles and the associated religious practices, we gain insights into the religious landscape of ancient Babylon and the rituals performed to honor these deities.

Nergal, the god of war and pestilence, played a vital role in Babylonian religion. As a deity associated with warfare, Nergal was invoked to grant victory in battles, protect warriors, and ensure the prosperity of the kingdom. Rituals dedicated to Nergal often involved the offering of sacrifices, such as animals or food, to appease and gain favor from the deity. Incantations, known as exorcisms, were also recited to ward off evil spirits and diseases associated with Nergal's domain. These rituals and incantations served to establish a connection with the deity and seek his assistance and protection.

Ereshkigal, the goddess of the underworld, held a position of immense significance in ancient Babylonian religion. Rituals dedicated to Ereshkigal aimed to honor and appease the goddess, as well as seek her guidance and protection in matters related to death, the afterlife, and the mysteries of the underworld. These rituals often took the form of funerary practices, such as burial ceremonies and the offering of food and drink to the deceased. Incantations and prayers were recited to invoke Ereshkigal's presence and seek her blessings. The purpose of these rituals and incantations was to establish a connection with the goddess and ensure a smooth transition for the departed souls into the realm of the dead.

To further your understanding of the roles of Nergal and Ereshkigal in ancient Babylonian religion and the associated rituals and incantations, consider the following exercises:

Research and analyze specific rituals dedicated to Nergal and Ereshkigal. Examine the texts, artifacts, and archaeological evidence associated with these rituals. Discuss the symbols, gestures, and objects used in these ceremonies and their significance.

Explore the use of incantations and prayers in Babylonian religious practices. Examine the linguistic and poetic aspects of these texts, identifying the formulas, invocations, and theophoric elements. Discuss the purpose and intended effects of these incantations and prayers in the context of communicating with the deities.

Reflect on the similarities and differences between the rituals and incantations dedicated to Nergal and Ereshkigal and those found in other religious traditions, such as ancient Egyptian or Greek practices. Discuss the common themes and underlying beliefs that transcend cultures and civilizations.

Imagine you are an ancient Babylonian priest or priestess responsible for conducting rituals dedicated to Nergal or Ereshkigal. Design a ritual ceremony, including the necessary preparations, offerings, incantations, and gestures, and explain the intended outcomes and significance of each element.

By engaging in these exercises, you will deepen your understanding of the roles of Nergal and Ereshkigal in Babylonian religion and gain insights into the rituals and incantations dedicated to these deities. This knowledge will allow you to appreciate the cultural and religious practices of ancient Babylon and the ways in which these rituals aimed to establish a connection with the divine.

Spells for Malevolent Intentions

While it is important to approach the subject of malevolent intentions with caution and ethical considerations, for educational purposes, we can explore some concepts related to ancient Babylonian magic and sorcery. It's important to note that these practices should not be performed or encouraged for harmful purposes. Understanding them in a historical and cultural context is crucial to developing a comprehensive knowledge of ancient Babylonian beliefs and practices. Here are 10 spells that were used or theorized to have been used in ancient Babylon:

Spell of Infliction: A spell aimed at causing harm or illness to a specific individual, using rituals, incantations, and possibly the manipulation of symbolic objects.

In ancient Babylonian culture, magic and sorcery were believed to possess the power to influence and manipulate various aspects of life, including the well-being of individuals. While most Babylonian magical practices were intended for positive purposes, there is evidence to suggest that spells of infliction were also employed. These spells were used with the intention of causing harm or illness to a targeted individual. It is crucial to approach this topic with caution, as engaging in malevolent practices goes against ethical considerations and the principles of harm none.

Why it might have been used:

Revenge: The spell of infliction may have been used as a means of seeking revenge or retribution against someone who had wronged the spellcaster. It was believed that by causing harm to the target, the spellcaster could restore a sense of justice or balance.

Protection or Defense: In certain cases, the spell of infliction might have been used as a defensive measure. If someone believed they were under threat or facing danger from another person, they may have resorted to these spells as a means of self-defense or protection.

Negative Reactions and Ethical Considerations:
Casting a spell of infliction carried potential negative consequences, both for the target and the spellcaster. Here are some possible repercussions that might have arisen:

Karmic Consequences: The concept of karma played a significant role in ancient Babylonian beliefs. It was believed that any harm inflicted upon others would eventually return to the spellcaster in some form. Casting a spell of infliction could create a negative karmic cycle, perpetuating harm and negativity in the spellcaster's life.

Social Isolation: Engaging in malevolent practices may have resulted in social isolation and condemnation from the community. The spellcaster might have faced ostracism and reputational damage due to their actions.

Guilt and Regret: Casting a spell of infliction, even in ancient times, would likely have evoked feelings of guilt and remorse. The spellcaster might have experienced inner turmoil and the burden of responsibility for the harm caused.

Backfire or Reversal: There was always the possibility that the spell of infliction could have backfired, causing harm or illness to the spellcaster instead. Ancient Babylonian texts contain warnings about the risks and potential unintended consequences of engaging in malevolent magic.

Curse of Misfortune: A curse designed to bring misfortune and calamity upon the target, affecting various aspects of their life such as relationships, health, and success.

In the realm of ancient Babylonian magic, curses were regarded as potent tools for invoking negative energy and directing it towards an individual. While the majority of Babylonian magical practices were aimed at positive outcomes, it is important to acknowledge the existence of curses and their potential ramifications. Casting a curse of misfortune was a deliberate act of inflicting harm upon another, and it is crucial to approach this topic with caution and ethical considerations.

Why it might have been used:

Retribution and Revenge: The curse of misfortune might have been employed as a means of seeking retribution against someone who had caused harm or injustice to the spellcaster. It was believed that by invoking misfortune upon the target, a sense of justice or balance could be restored.

Personal Gain or Jealousy: In some instances, individuals may have resorted to curses out of personal gain or envy. The curse of misfortune could be cast with the intention of hindering the success, happiness, or prosperity of another person, thereby elevating the spellcaster's own position.

Negative Reactions and Ethical Considerations:
Casting a curse of misfortune carried potential negative consequences, both for the target and the spellcaster. Here are some possible repercussions that might have arisen:

Karmic Consequences: In ancient Babylonian belief systems, the concept of karma played a significant role. It was understood that any harm caused to others would eventually return to the spellcaster in some form. Casting a curse of misfortune could perpetuate a cycle of negative energy, resulting in long-term repercussions for the spellcaster.

Guilt and Regret: Engaging in malevolent practices, such as casting curses, would likely have evoked feelings of guilt and remorse in the spellcaster. The burden of responsibility for the misfortune inflicted upon another person may have weighed heavily on their conscience.

Potential Backlash: There was always a risk that the curse of misfortune could have unintended consequences for the spellcaster as well. Ancient Babylonian texts cautioned about the potential backlash or negative effects that could befall those who engaged in malicious magic.

Social Consequences: Employing curses as a means of causing misfortune would likely have resulted in social isolation and condemnation from the community. The spellcaster may have faced rejection and alienation due to their actions.

Binding Spell: A ritualistic practice performed to restrict or hinder the actions or abilities of a person, preventing them from causing harm or interfering in certain matters.

Within the realm of ancient Babylonian magic, binding spells held a significant place in the repertoire of mystical practices. These spells were primarily employed as a defensive measure, aiming to neutralize the influence or potential harm caused by an individual. It is essential to approach the topic of binding spells with caution, recognizing both their historical context and the potential ethical concerns that arise from manipulating the will or freedom of others.

Why it might have been used:

Protection and Self-Defense: Binding spells were commonly used to protect oneself or others from individuals who posed a threat or engaged in harmful actions. By binding their abilities or limiting their influence, the spellcaster sought to create a barrier that prevented further harm.

Controlling Negative Influences: In some instances, binding spells were employed to control or restrict the actions of individuals who were causing disruption or interference in specific matters. By limiting their abilities to act against one's interests, the spellcaster aimed to regain control and restore harmony.

Negative Reactions and Ethical Considerations:
While binding spells were often used as defensive measures, it is important to consider the potential negative reactions and ethical implications associated with them:

Manipulation and Consent: Engaging in binding spells raises concerns regarding the manipulation of another person's will or freedom. It is crucial to respect individual autonomy and consider the implications of imposing limitations on others without their consent.

Unintended Consequences: The use of binding spells carries the risk of unintended consequences or unforeseen outcomes. It is possible that by restricting someone's abilities, the spellcaster may inadvertently disrupt natural processes or hinder personal growth.

Ethical Dilemmas: The practice of binding spells involves ethical dilemmas, as it delves into the realm of controlling and restricting the actions of others. These dilemmas raise questions about personal responsibility, the appropriate use of power, and the potential for abuse.

Energy Exchange and Karma: The manipulation of energy and the act of binding someone may have karmic consequences. The spellcaster must consider the potential repercussions of their actions, as the energy they send out into the universe can have a reciprocal effect.

It is crucial to approach the study of binding spells within the context of historical and cultural understanding, without advocating for their use in contemporary settings. The inclusion of this information in the textbook serves the purpose of educational exploration, allowing students to gain insights into ancient Babylonian beliefs and practices.

Hex of Confusion: A spell intended to cloud the mind and judgment of an individual, leading to confusion, indecision, and difficulties in making rational choices.

Within the realm of ancient Babylonian magic, the Hex of Confusion held a place among the spells designed to influence the thoughts and mental processes of individuals. It is important to approach the topic with caution, recognizing both its historical context and the potential ethical concerns that arise from manipulating the mental state of others.

Why it might have been used:

Personal Gain: The Hex of Confusion could have been employed by individuals seeking to gain an advantage over others. By clouding the judgment and decision-making abilities of a targeted individual, the spellcaster aimed to create a situation where their own interests would be favored.

Disruption and Chaos: In certain circumstances, the Hex of Confusion might have been used as a means of causing disruption and chaos. By inducing confusion and indecision, the spellcaster sought to create a state of uncertainty and disorder within the targeted individual's life or circumstances.

Negative Reactions and Ethical Considerations:
While the Hex of Confusion might have been used for personal gain or to cause disruption, it is important to consider the potential negative reactions and ethical implications associated with such practices:

Manipulation of Free Will: Engaging in spells that intentionally cloud someone's judgment raises concerns about manipulating their free will. It is crucial to respect individual autonomy and consider the ethical implications of tampering with another person's mental state without their consent.

Unintended Consequences: The use of the Hex of Confusion carries the risk of unintended consequences or unforeseen outcomes. The spellcaster must consider the potential collateral damage and the ripple effects that may extend beyond the targeted individual.

Harmful Intent: Employing spells with the intent to cause confusion and distress in others raises ethical dilemmas. It is important to evaluate the motives and intentions behind such actions, ensuring they align with principles of compassion, empathy, and ethical responsibility.

Personal Growth and Learning: Hindering someone's ability to make rational choices might impede their personal growth and development. It is essential to consider the potential negative impact on the individual's well-being and their journey of self-discovery.

Necromancy and Divination of the Dead

In the realm of ancient Babylonian occult practices, the art of communicating with and seeking guidance from the deceased played a significant role. Necromancy, the practice of divination through contact with the dead, held both religious and spiritual significance in ancient Babylonian culture. This chapter explores the beliefs, rituals, and methods associated with necromancy and divination of the dead, shedding light on the ancient Babylonian's fascination with the afterlife and the quest for insight and wisdom from departed souls.

Beliefs Surrounding the Afterlife

The Underworld and the Realm of the Dead

The Babylonian Concept of the Afterlife

In ancient Babylonian mythology and religious beliefs, the concept of the afterlife was intricately woven into the fabric of their worldview. The Babylonians held a deep belief in the continuation of existence after death and the existence of a realm specifically designated for the souls of the deceased. This realm, known as the underworld or Irkalla, held great significance in Babylonian cosmology and shaped their understanding of the spiritual journey beyond earthly life.

The Babylonians viewed the underworld as a mysterious and complex domain, existing beneath the earth's surface. It was believed to be a realm separate from the world of the living, where the souls of the departed resided. Irkalla was often depicted as a subterranean realm, filled with vast caverns, shadowy passages, and a somber atmosphere.

The belief in the existence of the underworld was rooted in the Babylonian perception of death as a transition rather than an absolute end. It was believed that after the physical body ceased to function, the soul embarked on a journey to the underworld, guided by specific rituals, funerary practices, and religious rites.

The Babylonians attributed great importance to the underworld as it played a crucial role in their cosmological understanding. They believed that the realm of Irkalla was ruled by the goddess Ereshkigal, who held absolute power and authority over the souls of the deceased. Ereshkigal was revered as a formidable figure, embodying the forces of death, decay, and transformation.

The concept of the underworld and its associated rituals and beliefs served multiple purposes in Babylonian society. Firstly, it provided a framework for understanding the nature of life, death, and the spiritual journey beyond the physical realm. It offered solace to individuals in the face of mortality, assuring them of an existence beyond the earthly plane.

Additionally, the belief in the underworld had a profound impact on the moral and ethical conduct of the Babylonians. They believed that one's actions in life would be judged and evaluated in the afterlife, determining the fate and the quality of existence in Irkalla. This belief system instilled a sense of accountability and encouraged individuals to live virtuous and righteous lives, understanding the potential consequences in the realm of the dead.

The mythology and rituals surrounding the underworld also played a significant role in funerary practices and burial customs. Elaborate rituals were performed to ensure a safe and successful journey for the departed souls. Funerary offerings and rites were conducted to provide assistance and provisions for the deceased on their voyage through the realms of the underworld.

It is important to note that the beliefs and practices regarding the afterlife in ancient Babylonian culture varied across different periods and regions. The concept of the underworld and its specific attributes evolved and transformed over time, reflecting the changing religious and cultural landscape of the Babylonian civilization.

In conclusion, the Babylonian concept of the afterlife and the belief in the underworld played a central role in their mythology and religious beliefs. The existence of Irkalla, the realm inhabited by the souls of the deceased, was considered a mysterious and significant domain. It shaped their understanding of life, death, and the spiritual journey beyond earthly existence. The belief in the underworld influenced their moral conduct, provided comfort in the face of mortality, and informed their funerary practices and rituals.

Irkalla: The Underworld in Babylonian Mythology

The Babylonians held a vivid and intricate vision of the underworld, known as Irkalla, which was situated below the surface of the earth. This subterranean realm was believed to be a complex and expansive domain that served as the abode for the souls of the deceased. Within Irkalla, the powerful goddess Ereshkigal reigned as the supreme authority, presiding over the destinies and experiences of the departed souls.

Ereshkigal held a significant role in Babylonian mythology and religious beliefs as the ruler of the underworld. She was revered as a formidable and fearsome deity, embodying the forces of death, decay, and transformation. In the pantheon of Babylonian gods and goddesses, Ereshkigal represented the somber and mysterious aspects of existence, symbolizing the necessary cycle of life and death.

As the queen of the underworld, Ereshkigal was responsible for upholding the laws and order of the afterlife. She enforced the rules and regulations that governed the fate and experiences of the deceased within Irkalla. It was believed that Ereshkigal possessed the power to reward or punish the souls based on their conduct during their earthly lives.

The Babylonians held a deep reverence and awe for Ereshkigal, recognizing her authority and influence over the souls of the dead. She was often depicted as a stern and formidable figure, clad in regal attire that represented her divine status. In Babylonian mythology, there were various myths and narratives that highlighted the power and significance of Ereshkigal, such as the famous myth of Inanna's descent into the underworld.

The role of Ereshkigal in the Babylonian conception of the afterlife was multifaceted. On one hand, she represented the somber and inevitable aspects of existence, reminding the living of the transient nature of life and the necessity of death. Her presence and authority in the underworld served as a reminder of the consequences of one's actions and the potential judgment awaiting them in the afterlife.

At the same time, Ereshkigal's role as the ruler of the underworld also encompassed compassion and mercy. It was believed that she had the power to provide solace and comfort to the souls in her realm, offering them respite and guidance in their journey beyond earthly life. In this sense, Ereshkigal symbolized the transformative nature of death and the potential for spiritual growth and enlightenment in the afterlife.

The belief in Ereshkigal and her dominion over the souls of the dead had a profound impact on Babylonian funerary practices and rituals. Elaborate ceremonies and offerings were conducted to honor and appease the goddess, seeking her favor and protection for the departed souls. These rituals aimed to ensure a smooth transition and a favorable destiny for the deceased within the realms of Irkalla.

In conclusion, the Babylonian concept of the underworld, Irkalla, was intricately tied to the powerful goddess Ereshkigal, who ruled over the realm of the dead. Her authority and influence shaped the beliefs and practices surrounding the afterlife in Babylonian culture. As the queen of the underworld, Ereshkigal enforced the laws and order of the afterlife, rewarding or punishing souls based on their earthly actions. Understanding the role of Ereshkigal provides valuable insights into the Babylonian perception of death, the cycle of life, and the transformative nature of the afterlife.

The Journey to the Underworld

According to Babylonian mythology, the journey to the underworld was not a straightforward or effortless endeavor. The souls of the deceased were believed to face a series of formidable challenges and trials that tested their strength, character, and worthiness before they could reach their final destination in the realm of the dead. These challenges held profound symbolic meaning, representing the necessary tests one must undergo to prove their eligibility for entry into the afterlife.

The Babylonian belief in the arduous journey to the underworld emphasized the notion that death was not simply a transition from one state of being to another, but a transformative process that required the soul to confront and overcome various obstacles. These challenges served as a means of purification and judgment, determining the fate and destiny of the deceased based on their responses and actions during these trials.

One of the prominent myths illustrating the challenges faced by the souls on their journey to the underworld is the epic of Gilgamesh. In this ancient Mesopotamian narrative, the hero Gilgamesh travels to the realm of the dead in search of immortality. Along the way, he encounters numerous trials and obstacles, including crossing a treacherous river, navigating through dark and perilous paths, and even confronting supernatural guardians. These challenges test his resolve, courage, and wisdom, ultimately shaping his understanding of mortality and the limitations of human existence.

The challenges faced by the souls on their journey to the underworld symbolized the ethical and moral aspects of life. It was believed that the souls had to demonstrate virtues such as righteousness, courage, and compassion to pass these tests successfully. Those who had led virtuous lives were more likely to navigate the challenges and reach a favorable destination in the realm of the dead, while those who had been morally compromised might face more difficult trials or even be denied entry altogether.

The purpose of these challenges was not to inflict unnecessary suffering but rather to ensure that the souls had undergone a transformative process and had developed the qualities necessary for their spiritual growth and evolution. The trials were seen as opportunities for the souls to reflect on their past actions, make amends, and learn important lessons that would shape their future existence in the afterlife.

It is important to note that the challenges and trials on the journey to the underworld were not solely punitive in nature. They also provided an opportunity for redemption and spiritual growth. Souls who demonstrated remorse, repentance, and a sincere desire for transformation could overcome their past shortcomings and earn a more favorable destiny in the realm of the dead.

In conclusion, according to Babylonian mythology, the journey to the underworld was fraught with challenges and trials that symbolized the tests of character and worthiness faced by the souls of the deceased. These challenges were seen as transformative opportunities for the souls to demonstrate virtues, learn important lessons, and undergo spiritual growth. The belief in the arduous journey underscored the Babylonian understanding of the afterlife as a realm where the moral and ethical aspects of one's earthly existence were weighed and judged.

Cosmological Beliefs and the Journey of the Soul

The Babylonians possessed a multifaceted comprehension of the journey undertaken by the soul after death. They perceived death as the separation of the soul from the physical body, marking the commencement of a hazardous expedition towards the underworld. This expedition was not a passive transition but rather an arduous and transformative journey that demanded the soul to confront a multitude of obstacles and endure rigorous trials.

The belief in the soul's journey to the underworld was grounded in the Babylonian understanding of the afterlife as a distinct realm with its own laws, rulers, and cosmic order. It was believed that the soul, upon departing the body, embarked on a treacherous path, guided by rituals, incantations, and the intercession of deities. The purpose of this journey was to reach the realm of the dead, a realm governed by the powerful goddess Ereshkigal.

The challenges and tests encountered by the soul during its journey held significant symbolic meaning. They represented the moral and spiritual growth that the soul was expected to undergo in preparation for its ultimate destiny in the afterlife. These challenges were not arbitrary or random; rather, they served as opportunities for the soul to demonstrate its worthiness, integrity, and adherence to ethical principles.

The trials faced by the soul on its journey were varied and demanding. They could include crossing perilous rivers, navigating through treacherous landscapes, and confronting guardians or divine beings. Each challenge represented a different aspect of the soul's character and virtue, assessing its ability to navigate moral dilemmas, exhibit courage in the face of adversity, and uphold principles of justice and righteousness.

It is important to note that the purpose of these trials was not solely punitive but also redemptive and transformative. The challenges were designed to refine and purify the soul, enabling it to shed the imperfections and negative influences accumulated during its earthly existence. By overcoming these trials, the soul could achieve a state of moral perfection and attain a favorable destiny in the realm of the dead.

The belief in the soul's journey to the underworld reflected the Babylonian understanding of life as a continuous process of growth and evolution. It emphasized the importance of ethical conduct, moral choices, and spiritual development during one's earthly life. The challenges and tests encountered on the journey served as reminders of the consequences of one's actions and the need for personal accountability.

In conclusion, the Babylonians held a complex understanding of the journey of the soul after death. They believed that the soul embarked on a perilous and transformative journey towards the underworld, facing numerous challenges and tests along the way. These trials symbolized the soul's moral and spiritual growth, offering opportunities for redemption, purification, and the attainment of a favorable destiny in the afterlife. The belief in the soul's journey underscored the Babylonian view of life as a process of continual moral and spiritual evolution.

Judgment and Accountability

In the intricate cosmology of ancient Babylon, the concept of accountability for one's actions extended beyond earthly life. According to Babylonian belief, upon entering the realm of the dead, the soul of the deceased would face a profound evaluation known as the judgment process. This process was a pivotal moment that determined the soul's fate and the nature of its existence in the afterlife.

During the judgment process, the soul would come before a council of deities, who served as impartial judges. These divine beings possessed omniscience and wisdom, enabling them to assess the moral conduct and deeds of the departed soul during its earthly life. The purpose of this judgment was to determine the soul's eligibility for rewards or punishments in the afterlife, based on its adherence to ethical principles and the consequences of its actions.

The evaluation of the soul's deeds encompassed a comprehensive analysis of its thoughts, words, and deeds while alive. The council of deities scrutinized the individual's behavior, taking into account factors such as compassion, honesty, generosity, and adherence to societal norms and divine laws. The soul's intentions and motivations were also considered in the judgment process, as the Babylonians believed that true righteousness extended beyond mere external actions.

The judgment process was guided by a sense of justice and fairness, ensuring that each soul would be held accountable for its choices and actions. The deities involved in the judgment process acted as impartial arbiters, weighing the merits and transgressions of the deceased with meticulous scrutiny. This process was believed to reflect the cosmic order and divine justice, as the Babylonians believed in the existence of an inherent moral balance in the universe.

Based on the outcome of the judgment, the soul would be assigned a specific fate in the afterlife. For those deemed righteous and virtuous, a variety of rewards awaited them, including eternal bliss, reunion with loved ones, and the opportunity to dwell in the presence of benevolent deities. Conversely, souls found guilty of moral transgressions and wickedness would face various forms of punishment, such as torment, separation from loved ones, or even annihilation.

It is important to note that the judgment process in Babylonian cosmology served as a means of reinforcing the significance of ethical behavior and personal responsibility. It underscored the belief that one's actions during earthly life had consequences that extended beyond death. This belief system aimed to motivate individuals to lead virtuous lives, understanding that their deeds would be subject to scrutiny and evaluation in the afterlife.

In conclusion, the Babylonians held a profound belief in the accountability of the soul for its actions during earthly life. The judgment process that the deceased underwent in the realm of the dead was a crucial aspect of Babylonian cosmology. Through the evaluation of the soul's moral conduct and deeds, a council of deities determined the soul's fate in the afterlife, whether it would be rewarded or punished. This belief emphasized the importance of ethical behavior and personal responsibility, as actions during earthly life were believed to shape the destiny of the soul in the cosmic order established by the divine.

Challenges and Trials in the Underworld

Within the intricate belief system of ancient Babylon, the journey through the underworld was not a straightforward passage but a treacherous odyssey filled with challenges and trials. These obstacles were seen as necessary elements in the soul's spiritual evolution, serving to test its resolve, virtue, and readiness for ultimate transformation. They symbolized the arduous journey towards spiritual enlightenment, purification, and redemption.

One of the significant challenges encountered during the journey through the underworld involved confronting formidable guardians. These guardians were often depicted as fearsome beings, endowed with supernatural powers and tasked with safeguarding the entrance to the realm of the dead. Their purpose was to test the worthiness of the soul seeking passage, ensuring that only those deemed deserving and prepared could proceed. These encounters demanded courage, determination, and the display of moral strength, as the soul had to prove its readiness to face the unknown.

Another trial on the journey through the underworld involved the crossing of treacherous rivers. These rivers, such as the River of Death or the River of Suffering, symbolized the barriers between the realm of the living and the realm of the dead. They represented the threshold between the earthly existence and the afterlife. Crossing these treacherous waters required the soul to navigate through dangerous currents, resist temptation, and demonstrate resilience in the face of adversity.

Furthermore, the soul would encounter various hardships and ordeals during its journey, mirroring the challenges faced in life. These difficulties tested the soul's fortitude, determination, and commitment to spiritual growth. They could include enduring physical or emotional pain, facing personal fears and inner demons, or undergoing transformative experiences that challenged the soul's preconceived notions and attachments.

The purpose of these trials within Babylonian belief was multifaceted. They served as a means of purification, allowing the soul to shed its earthly attachments, vices, and impurities in preparation for a higher state of existence. Through these challenges, the soul was provided with opportunities for self-reflection, self-discovery, and personal growth. The journey through the underworld was seen as a transformative process, wherein the soul could learn valuable lessons, confront its limitations, and ultimately evolve spiritually.

While these trials were undoubtedly demanding, their underlying purpose was not to inflict suffering or punishment upon the soul. Rather, they were intended to facilitate the soul's growth, enlightenment, and redemption. By overcoming these obstacles and emerging triumphant, the soul would be prepared to ascend to higher realms, attaining a state of greater spiritual awareness, and experiencing a deeper connection with divine forces.

It is important to note that the trials within Babylonian mythology should not be interpreted solely as physical or literal challenges. They encompassed a symbolic dimension, representing the inner struggles, moral dilemmas, and transformative experiences that individuals encounter on their spiritual journeys. These trials were metaphors for the hardships and tests faced in life, emphasizing the necessity of perseverance, resilience, and moral strength in the pursuit of spiritual growth and enlightenment.

In summary, according to Babylonian belief, the journey through the underworld was a profound and arduous process, filled with challenges and trials. These obstacles tested the soul's resolve, virtue, and readiness for transformation. By confronting formidable guardians, crossing treacherous rivers, and enduring various hardships, the soul embarked on a path of spiritual enlightenment and purification. These trials served as symbolic representations of the soul's inner struggles and its journey towards redemption and higher states of consciousness.

Eternal Rest and Existence in the Underworld

Once the soul had successfully journeyed through the trials of the underworld and underwent judgment, a new phase of existence awaited it. According to Babylonian belief, the soul would find eternal rest and peace in a realm within the underworld, where it would join the company of other deceased individuals. This realm of existence was intricately linked to the deeds and moral character exhibited by the soul during its earthly life.

In Babylonian cosmology, it was understood that the soul's fate in the afterlife was determined by the judgment it received from a council of deities. This judgment assessed the soul's actions, intentions, and moral conduct during its time on Earth. The council would weigh the balance of the soul's virtues and transgressions, considering factors such as righteousness, benevolence, honesty, and adherence to social and religious norms.

Based on the outcome of this judgment, the soul would be assigned a specific place or state within the underworld. Those souls deemed righteous and deserving of reward would enter a realm of bliss, where they could experience eternal peace and contentment. This realm was often described as a serene and idyllic paradise, where the righteous souls could enjoy the company of like-minded individuals and engage in activities that brought them joy and fulfillment. It was a place where the soul could find solace and liberation from the struggles and tribulations of the earthly existence.

Conversely, souls that were deemed to have led lives characterized by wrongdoing, immorality, or malevolence would face a different fate. These souls would be consigned to a realm or state reflective of their deeds and moral character. The nature of this realm varied, but it was often described as a place of punishment, suffering, or unfulfilled desires. The purpose of such a state was to serve as a means of rectification or atonement, allowing the soul to reconcile and purify itself from the negative influences and actions of its earthly life.

It is important to note that the Babylonian belief in the afterlife and the realms within the underworld was complex and multifaceted. The concept of eternal rest and peace for the righteous souls and punishment for the unrighteous souls reflected the Babylonians' moral framework and their understanding of divine justice. It provided a system of accountability and reward, reinforcing the importance of leading a virtuous and righteous life.

The notion of finding eternal rest and peace in the afterlife resonated deeply with the Babylonians, offering solace and hope in the face of mortality. It provided a sense of continuity and purpose beyond the earthly realm, assuring individuals that their actions and moral character mattered beyond their earthly existence. This belief in the afterlife served as a motivating force for individuals to strive for righteousness, seek moral integrity, and fulfill their societal and religious obligations.

In summary, according to Babylonian belief, once the soul successfully journeyed through the trials and received judgment in the underworld, it would find eternal rest and peace in a realm suited to its deeds and moral character. The righteous souls would enter a realm of bliss, experiencing joy, and fulfillment, while the unrighteous souls would face a realm reflective of their transgressions, serving as a means of rectification and purification. This belief system provided the Babylonians with a framework of divine justice and accountability, reinforcing the significance of leading a virtuous and righteous life.

Communication with the Deceased

In ancient Babylonian culture, the belief in communication with the dead held a profound significance. The Babylonians held the belief that through certain practices and rituals, they could establish a connection with deceased ancestors and revered figures from the past. This communication was seen as a means to access ancestral wisdom, seek guidance, and receive insights into various aspects of life.

The Babylonians regarded their ancestors with reverence and believed that the deceased retained knowledge and experiences that could be shared with the living. Seeking advice and guidance from the deceased was not only a means to honor and remember their ancestors but also a way to tap into a vast reservoir of wisdom accumulated over generations.

This belief in communication with the dead had deep cultural and religious roots. The Babylonians placed great importance on maintaining a connection with their ancestral lineage, as it provided a sense of continuity and belonging. Ancestral worship played a central role in their religious practices, as they believed that the spirits of their ancestors continued to exist and influence the lives of the living.

The ability to communicate with the dead was considered a sacred and mystical practice. It required specific rituals, incantations, and mediums through which the living could establish a connection with the spiritual realm. Babylonian priests and practitioners of divination and necromancy played a vital role in facilitating these communications, acting as intermediaries between the living and the deceased.

The act of seeking advice from deceased ancestors and revered figures held cultural and religious significance in ancient Babylonian society. It was believed that the wisdom and guidance received from the deceased could help individuals make informed decisions, navigate challenges, and gain insights into matters of personal, familial, and communal importance.

The practice of communicating with the dead was not only limited to personal matters but also extended to seeking guidance in religious and political affairs. The Babylonians believed that their ancestors possessed a deep understanding of the gods and the workings of the divine realm. Consulting with the deceased was thus seen as a means to gain insights into religious rituals, divine will, and the overall well-being of the community.

While the belief in communication with the dead provided a sense of connection and guidance, it also carried ethical considerations and potential pitfalls. The Babylonians understood the importance of approaching such practices with respect and caution. There was a recognition that not all spirits or entities encountered in the spiritual realm were benevolent or truthful. Therefore, it was essential to employ proper rituals, protective measures, and discernment when engaging in communication with the deceased.

In conclusion, the Babylonian belief in communication with the dead offered a means to access ancestral wisdom and seek guidance from revered figures. This belief had deep cultural and religious significance, providing a connection to the past, honoring ancestors, and seeking insights into various aspects of life. The practice of communicating with the deceased required specific rituals and mediums and was carried out by priests and practitioners skilled in divination and necromancy. However, it was essential to approach these practices with caution and discernment, recognizing both the potential benefits and the ethical considerations involved in seeking advice from the spiritual realm.

Dark Magic and Forbidden Arts

Within the realm of ancient Babylonian culture, alongside the prevalent beliefs and practices, there existed a shadowy undercurrent of dark magic and forbidden arts. These practices delved into the manipulation of souls, the use of blood magic, and the performance of rituals that were deemed off-limits and taboo. While these aspects are not widely discussed or openly embraced, it is crucial to explore and understand them within the context of ancient Babylonian culture.

Dark magic encompassed a range of practices that sought to harness and manipulate supernatural forces for personal gain, often employing methods that were considered morally questionable or dangerous. One such practice was the manipulation of souls, which involved the ability to control or influence the essence of an individual's being. This manipulation was believed to grant power over others, but it carried significant ethical considerations and potential consequences.

Blood magic, another aspect of dark magic, involved the use of blood as a potent and symbolic medium for rituals and spellcasting. The Babylonians believed that blood held immense power and served as a conduit between the physical and spiritual realms. Through intricate rituals and incantations, practitioners sought to tap into this power, often at great risk to themselves and those involved. The use of blood magic was associated with the invocation of deities and the manipulation of life forces, leading to potential consequences that extended beyond the immediate results of the spells.

Forbidden rituals were practices that were strictly prohibited or restricted within the Babylonian culture. These rituals often involved the invocation of malevolent entities, the breaking of sacred taboos, or the manipulation of forces that were deemed too dangerous to be tampered with. They were considered highly risky, both for the practitioner and for the overall balance and harmony of the spiritual realm. The intricate nature of these rituals required precise knowledge of symbolism, incantations, and ceremonial practices.

It is crucial to note that the use of dark magic in ancient Babylonian culture carried significant dangers and ethical considerations. While it provided access to formidable power and control, it often came at a high price. Engaging in dark magic was viewed as a violation of the natural order and could result in severe consequences for the practitioner and those involved. The manipulation of souls, for instance, not only infringed upon the autonomy of individuals but also disrupted the delicate balance of the spiritual realm, potentially inviting malevolent forces and chaos.

The use of blood magic, with its reliance on the life force contained within blood, carried the risk of unintended side effects and unforeseen repercussions. It was believed that the misuse or abuse of blood magic could lead to imbalances in the spiritual and physical realms, as well as the corruption of the practitioner's own soul. Forbidden rituals, with their disregard for established norms and sacred boundaries, often invited the attention of dark entities and could result in unintended harm to both the practitioner and innocent parties involved.

Within ancient Babylonian culture, the practice of dark magic and the engagement in forbidden arts were generally discouraged and viewed with caution. They were seen as deviations from the harmonious and ethical approach to spiritual practices that characterized the culture as a whole. Nevertheless, it is important to acknowledge the existence of these practices within the historical and cultural context of ancient Babylonian society, as they shed light on the complexities of their belief systems and the wide range of human spiritual exploration.

In conclusion, dark magic and forbidden arts were part of the mystical tapestry of ancient Babylonian culture, delving into practices such as soul manipulation, blood magic, and forbidden rituals. These practices were fraught with dangers, ethical considerations, and potential consequences that extended beyond immediate results. While they were not widely embraced, understanding these aspects within their historical and cultural context provides insights into the intricacies of ancient Babylonian beliefs and the diverse avenues of spiritual exploration present in their society.

www.ingramcontent.com/pod-product-compliance
Lightning Source LLC
Chambersburg PA
CBHW060413010526
44107CB00006B/677